THE HOME UNIVERSITY LIBRARY
OF MODERN KNOWLEDGE

74

A HISTORY OF
FREEDOM OF THOUGHT

A History of
Freedom of Thought

J. B. BURY
with an Epilogue by
H. J. BLACKHAM

Second Edition

GREENWOOD PRESS, PUBLISHERS
WESTPORT, CONNECTICUT

Library of Congress Cataloging in Publication Data

Bury, John Bagnell, 1861-1927.
    A history of freedom of thought.

    Reprint of the 1952 ed. published by G. Cumberlege at
the Oxford University Press, London, New York, which was
issued as no. 74 of the Home university library of modern
knowledge.
    Bibliography: p.
    Includes index.
    1. Free thought--History. 2. Rationalism--History.
I. Title.
BL2750.B8 1975   211'.4   74-30844
ISBN 0-8371-7935-1

This edition published in 1952 by Oxford University Press,
London

This reprint has been authorized by the Clarendon Press Oxford

Reprinted in 1975 by Greenwood Press,
a division of Williamhouse-Regency Inc.

Library of Congress Catalog Card Number 74-30844

ISBN 0-8371-7935-1

Printed in the United States of America

211.4
B975

CONTENTS

PREFACE TO SECOND EDITION

Bury's stirring essay was written in 1912. He died in 1927. If one were to continue his story by producing the lines of his penultimate chapter, the last of his narrative, and tell the sequel in biblical criticism, anthropology, organized rationalism, and religions of progress, the result would be derisory in its contemporary irrelevance. The Epilogue (which is written from Bury's point of view) revives the immediacy of the earlier chapters, which to the reader of 1913 could have been only a tale of old unhappy far-off things. The *dénouement* is undone, but the unity of the action still threads its simplicity through the complications of the theme. Progress is a difficult possibility; nothing is achieved once for all.

Bury's text and footnotes and his bibliography are reprinted without alteration. Anything that is obviously out of date is not likely to mislead. A few footnotes (which bear my initials) have been added, mainly on points which require revision in the light of more recent research. For one or two of these I am indebted to the advice of Dr. Roland Bainton of Yale, but responsibility for all the statements made is mine alone.

1951   H. J. BLACKHAM

Chapter I

INTRODUCTORY:

FREEDOM OF THOUGHT AND THE FORCES AGAINST IT

IT IS a common saying that thought is free. A man can never be hindered from thinking whatever he chooses so long as he conceals what he thinks. The working of his mind is limited only by the bounds of his experience and the power of his imagination. But this natural liberty of private thinking is of little value. It is unsatisfactory and even painful to the thinker himself, if he is not permitted to communicate his thoughts to others, and it is obviously of no value to his neighbours. Moreover it is extremely difficult to hide thoughts that have any power over the mind. If a man's thinking leads him to call in question ideas and customs which regulate the behaviour of those about him, to reject beliefs which they hold, to see better ways of life than those they follow, it is almost impossible for him, if he is convinced of the truth of his own reasoning, not to betray by silence, chance words, or general attitude that he is different from them and does not share their opinions. Some have preferred, like Socrates, some would prefer to-day, to face death rather than conceal their thoughts. Thus freedom of thought, in any valuable sense, includes freedom of speech.

At present, in the most civilized countries, freedom of speech is taken as a matter of course and seems a perfectly simple thing. We are so accustomed to it that we look on it as a natural right. But this right has been acquired only in quite recent times, and the way to its attainment has lain through lakes of blood. It has taken centuries to persuade the most enlightened peoples that liberty to publish one's opinions and to discuss all questions is a good and not a bad thing. Human societies (there are some brilliant exceptions) have been generally opposed to freedom of thought, or, in other words, to new ideas, and it is easy to see why.

The average brain is naturally lazy and tends to take the line of least resistance. The mental world of the ordinary man consists of beliefs which he has accepted without questioning and to which he is firmly attached; he is instinctively hostile to anything which would upset the established order of this familiar world. A new idea, inconsistent with some of the beliefs which he holds, means the necessity of re-arranging his mind; and this process is laborious, requiring a painful expenditure of brain-energy. To him and his fellows, who form the vast majority, new ideas, and opinions which cast doubt on established beliefs and institutions, seem evil because they are disagreeable.

The repugnance due to mere mental laziness is increased by a positive feeling of fear. The conservative instinct hardens into the conservative doctrine that the foundations of society are endangered by any alterations in the structure. It is only recently that men have been abandoning the belief that the welfare of a State depends on rigid stability and on the preservation of its traditions and institutions unchanged. Wherever that belief prevails, novel opinions are felt to be dangerous as well as annoying, and any one who asks inconvenient questions about the why and the wherefore of accepted principles is considered a pestilent person.

The conservative instinct, and the conservative doctrine which is its consequence, are strengthened by superstition. If the social structure, including the whole body of customs and opinions, is associated intimately with religious belief and is supposed to be under divine patronage, criticism of the social order savours of impiety, while criticism of the religious belief is a direct challenge to the wrath of supernatural powers.

The psychological motives which produce a conservative spirit hostile to new ideas are reinforced by the active opposition of certain powerful sections of the community, such as a class, a caste, or a priesthood, whose interests are bound up with the maintenance of the established order and the ideas on which it rests.

Let us suppose, for instance, that a people believes that solar eclipses are signs employed by their Deity for the special purpose of communicating useful information to them, and that a clever man discovers the true cause of eclipses. His compatriots in the first place dislike his discovery because they find it very difficult to reconcile with their other ideas; in the second place, it disturbs them, because it upsets an arrangement which they consider highly advantageous to their community; finally, it frightens them, as an offence to their Divinity. The priests, one of whose functions is to interpret the divine signs, are alarmed and enraged at a doctrine which menaces their power.

In prehistoric days, these motives, operating strongly, must have made change slow in communities which progressed, and hindered some communities from progressing at all. But they have continued to operate more or less throughout history, obstructing knowledge and progress. We can observe them at work to-day even in the most advanced societies, where they have no longer the power to arrest development or repress the publication of revolutionary opinions. We still meet people who consider a new idea an annoyance and probably a danger. Of those to whom socialism is repugnant, how many are there who have never examined the arguments for and against it, but turn away in disgust simply because the notion disturbs their mental universe and implies a drastic criticism on the order of things to which they are accustomed? And how many are there who would refuse to consider any proposals for altering our imperfect matrimonial institutions, because such an idea offends a mass of prejudice associated with religious sanctions? They may be right or not, but if they are, it is not their fault. They are actuated by the same motives which were a bar to progress in primitive societies. The existence of people of this mentality, reared in an atmosphere of freedom, side by side with others who are always looking out for new ideas and regretting that there are not more about, enables us to realize how, when public opinion was formed by the views of such men, thought was fettered and the impediments to knowledge enormous.

Although the liberty to publish one's opinions on any subject without regard to authority or the prejudices of one's neighbours is now a well-established principle, I imagine that only the minority of those who would be ready to fight to the death rather than surrender it could defend it on rational grounds. We are apt to take for granted that freedom of speech is a natural and inalienable birthright of man, and perhaps to think that this is a sufficient answer to all that can be said on the other side. But it is difficult to see how such a right can be established.[1]

If a man has any 'natural rights', the right to preserve his life and the right to reproduce his kind are certainly such. Yet human societies impose upon their members restrictions in the exercise of both these rights. A starving man is prohibited from taking food which belongs to somebody else. Promiscuous reproduction is restricted by various laws or customs. It is admitted that society is justified in restricting these elementary rights, because without such restrictions an ordered society could not exist. If then we concede that the expression of opinion is a right of the same kind, it is

[1]Since the adoption in 1948 by the General Assembly of the U.N. of a Universal Declaration of Human Rights which provides (Articles 18 and 19) for freedom of thought, conscience, and religion, and freedom of opinion and expression, these rights are at least widely acknowledged, if not yet established by international law.—H.J.B.

impossible to contend that on this ground it can claim immunity from interference or that society acts unjustly in regulating it. But the concession is too large. For whereas in the other cases the limitations affect the conduct of every one, restrictions on freedom of opinion affect only the comparatively small number who have any opinions, revolutionary or unconventional, to express. The truth is that no valid argument can be founded on the conception of natural rights, because it involves an untenable theory of the relations between society and its members.

On the other hand, those who have the responsibility of governing a society can argue that it is as incumbent on them to prohibit the circulation of pernicious opinions as to prohibit any anti-social actions. They can argue that a man may do far more harm by propagating anti-social doctrines than by stealing his neighbour's horse or making love to his neighbour's wife. They are responsible for the welfare of the State, and if they are convinced that an opinion is dangerous, by menacing the political, religious, or moral assumptions on which the society is based, it is their duty to protect society against it, as against any other danger.

The true answer to this argument for limiting freedom of thought will appear in due course. It was far from obvious. A long time was needed to arrive at the conclusion that coercion of opinion is a mistake, and only a part of the world is yet convinced. That conclusion, so far as I can judge, is the most important ever reached by men. It was the issue of a continuous struggle between authority and reason—the subject of this volume. The word *authority* requires some comment.

If you ask somebody how he knows something, he may say, 'I have it on good authority,' or, 'I read it in a book,' or, 'It is a matter of common knowledge,' or, 'I learned it at school.' Any of these replies means that he has accepted information from others, trusting in their knowledge, without verifying their statements or thinking the matter out for himself. And the greater part of most men's knowledge and beliefs is of this kind, taken without verification from their parents, teachers, acquaintances, books, newspapers. When an English boy learns French, he takes the conjugations and the meanings of the words on the authority of his teacher or his grammar. The fact that in a certain place, marked on the map, there is a populous city called Calcutta, is for most people a fact accepted on authority. So is the existence of Napoleon or Julius Caesar. Familiar astronomical facts are known only in the same way, except by those who have studied astronomy. It is obvious that every one's knowledge would be very limited indeed, if we were not justified in accepting facts on the authority of others.

But we are justified only under one condition. The facts which we can safely accept must be capable of demonstration or verification. The examples I have given belong to this class. The boy can verify when he goes to France or is able to read a French book that the facts which he took on authority are true. I am confronted every day with evidence which proves to me that, if I took the trouble, I could verify the existence of Calcutta for myself. I cannot convince myself in this way of the existence of Napoleon, but if I have doubts about it, a simple process of reasoning shows me that there are hosts of facts which are incompatible with his non-existence. I have no doubt that the earth is some 93 millions of miles distant from the sun, because all astronomers agree that it has been demonstrated, and their agreement is only explicable on the supposition that this has been demonstrated and that, if I took the trouble to work out the calculation, I should reach the same result.

But all our mental furniture is not of this kind. The thoughts of the average man consist not only of facts open to verification, but also of many beliefs and opinions which he has accepted on authority and cannot verify or prove. Belief in the Trinity depends on the authority of the Church and is clearly of a different order from belief in the existence of Calcutta. We cannot go behind the authority and verify or prove it. If we accept it, we do so because we have such implicit faith in the authority that we credit its assertions though incapable of proof.

The distinction may seem so obvious as to be hardly worth making. But it is important to be quite clear about it. The primitive man who had learned from his elders that there were bears in the hills and likewise evil spirits, soon verified the former statement by seeing a bear, but if he did not happen to meet an evil spirit, it did not occur to him, unless he was a prodigy, that there was a distinction between the two statements; he would rather have argued, if he argued at all, that as his tribesmen were right about the bears they were sure to be right also about the spirits. In the Middle Ages a man who believed on authority that there is a city called Constantinople and that comets are portents signifying divine wrath, would not distinguish the nature of the evidence in the two cases. You may still sometimes hear arguments amounting to this: since I believe in Calcutta on authority, am I not entitled to believe in the Devil on authority?

Now people at all times have been commanded or expected or invited to accept on authority alone—the authority, for instance, of public opinion, or a Church, or a sacred book—doctrines which are not proved or are not capable of proof. Most beliefs about nature and man, which were not founded on scientific observation, have served directly or indirectly religious and social interests, and hence they have been protected by force against the criticisms of persons who have the inconvenient habit of using their reason. Nobody minds if his neighbour disbelieves a demonstrable fact. If a sceptic denies that Napoleon existed, or that water is composed of oxygen and hydrogen, he causes amusement or ridicule. But if he denies doctrines which cannot be demonstrated, such as the existence of a personal God or the immortality of the soul, he incurs serious disapprobation and at one time he might have been put to death. Our mediaeval friend would have only been called a fool if he doubted the existence of Constantinople, but if he had questioned the significance of comets he might have got into trouble. It is possible that if he had been so mad as to deny the existence of Jerusalem he would not have escaped with ridicule, for Jerusalem is mentioned in the Bible.

In the Middle Ages a large field was covered by beliefs which authority claimed to impose as true, and reason was warned off the ground. But reason cannot recognize arbitrary prohibitions or barriers, without being untrue to herself. The universe of experience is her province, and as its parts are all linked together and interdependent, it is impossible for her to recognize any territory on which she may not tread, or to surrender any of her rights to an authority whose credentials she has not examined and approved.

The uncompromising assertion by reason of her absolute rights throughout the whole domain of thought is termed *rationalism*, and the slight stigma which is still attached to the word reflects the bitterness of the struggle between reason and the forces arrayed against her. The term is limited to the field of theology, because it was in that field that the self-assertion of reason was most violently and pertinaciously opposed. In the same way *free thought*, the refusal of thought to be controlled by any authority but its own, has a definitely theological reference. Throughout the conflict, authority has had great advantages. At any time the people who really care about reason have been a small minority, and probably will be so for a long time to come. Reason's only weapon has been argument. Authority has employed physical and moral violence, legal coercion and social displeasure. Sometimes she has attempted to use the sword of her adversary, thereby wounding herself. Indeed the weakest point in the strategical position of authority was that her champions, being human, could not help making use of reasoning processes and the result was that they were divided among themselves. This gave reason her chance. Operating, as it were, in the enemy's camp and professedly in the enemy's cause, she was preparing her own victory.

It may be objected that there is a legitimate domain for authority, consisting of doctrines which lie outside human experience and therefore cannot be proved or verified, but at the same time cannot be disproved. Of course, any number of propositions can be invented which cannot be disproved, and it is open to any one who possesses exuberant faith to believe them; but no one will maintain that they all deserve credence so long as their falsehood is not demonstrated. And if only some deserve credence, who, except reason, is to decide which? If the reply is, Authority, we are confronted by the difficulty that many beliefs backed by authority have been finally disproved and are universally abandoned. Yet some people speak as if we were not justified in rejecting a theological doctrine unless we can prove it false. But the burden of proof does not lie upon the rejecter. I remember a conversation in which, when some disrespectful remark was made about hell, a loyal friend of that establishment said triumphantly, 'But, absurd as it may seem, you cannot disprove it.' If you were told that in a certain planet revolving round Sirius there is a race of donkeys who talk the English language and spend their time in discussing eugenics, you could not disprove the statement, but would it, on that account, have any claim to be believed? Some minds would be prepared to accept it, if it were reiterated often enough, through the potent force of suggestion. This force, exercised largely by emphatic repetition (the theoretical basis, as has been observed, of the modern practice of advertising), has played a great part in establishing authoritative opinions and propagating religious creeds. Reason fortunately is able to avail herself of the same help.

The following sketch is confined to Western civilization. It begins with Greece and attempts to indicate the chief phases. It is the merest introduction to a vast and intricate subject, which, treated adequately, would involve not only the history of religion, of the Churches, of heresies, of persecution, but also the history of philosophy, of the natural sciences and of political theories. From the sixteenth century to the French Revolution nearly all important historical events bore in some way on the struggle for freedom of thought. It would require a lifetime to calculate, and many books to describe, all the directions and interactions of the intellectual and social forces which, since the fall of ancient civilization, have hindered and helped the emancipation of reason. All one can do, all one could do even in a much bigger volume than this, is to indicate the general course of the struggle and dwell on some particular aspects which the writer may happen to have specially studied.

Chapter II

REASON FREE: GREECE AND ROME

WHEN we are asked to specify the debt which civilization owes to the Greeks, their achievements in literature and art naturally occur to us first of all. But a truer answer may be that our deepest gratitude is due to them as the originators of liberty of thought and discussion. For this freedom of spirit was not only the condition of their speculations in philosophy, their progress in science, their experiments in political institutions; it was also a condition of their literary and artistic excellence. Their literature, for instance, could not have been what it is if they had been debarred from free criticism of life. But apart from what they actually accomplished, even if they had not achieved the wonderful things they did in most of the realms of human activity, their assertion of the principle of liberty would place them in the highest rank among the benefactors of the race; for it was one of the greatest steps in human progress.

We do not know enough about the earliest history of the Greeks to explain how it was that they attained their free outlook upon the world and came to possess the will and courage to set no bounds to the range of their criticism and curiosity. We have to take this character as a fact. But it must be remembered that the Greeks consisted of a large number of separate peoples, who varied largely in temper, customs and traditions, though they had important features common to all. Some were conservative, or backward, or unintellectual compared with others. In this chapter 'the Greeks' does not mean all the Greeks, but only those who count most in the history of civilization, especially the Ionians and Athenians.

Ionia in Asia Minor was the cradle of free speculation. The history of European science and European philosophy begins in Ionia. Here (in the sixth and fifth centuries B.C.) the early philosophers by using their reason sought to penetrate into the origin and structure of the world. They could not of course free their minds entirely from received notions, but they began the work of destroying orthodox views and religious faiths. Xenophanes may specially be named among these pioneers of thought (though he was not the most important or the ablest), because the toleration of his teaching illustrates the freedom of the atmosphere in which these men lived. He went about from city to city, calling in question on moral grounds the popular beliefs about the gods and goddesses, and ridiculing the anthropomorphic conceptions which the Greeks had formed of their divinities. 'If oxen had hands and the capacities of men, they would make gods in the shape of oxen.' This attack on received theology was an attack on the veracity of the old poets, especially Homer, who was considered the highest authority on mythology. Xenophanes criticized him severely for ascribing to the gods acts which, committed by men, would be considered highly disgraceful. We do not hear that any attempt was made to restrain him from thus assailing traditional beliefs and branding Homer as immoral. We must remember that the Homeric poems were never supposed to be the word of God. It has been said that Homer was the Bible of the Greeks. The remark exactly misses the truth. The Greeks fortunately had no Bible, and this fact was both an expression and an important condition of their freedom. Homer's poems were secular, not religious, and it may be noted that they are freer from immorality and savagery than sacred books that one could mention. Their authority was immense; but it was not binding like the authority of a sacred book and so Homeric criticism was never hampered like Biblical criticism.

In this connexion, notice may be taken of another expression and condition of freedom, the absence of sacerdotalism. The priests of the temples never became powerful castes, tyrannizing over the community in their own interests and able to silence voices raised against religious beliefs. The civil authorities kept the general control of public worship in their own hands, and, if some priestly families might have considerable influence, yet as a rule the priests were virtually State servants whose voice carried no weight except concerning the technical details of ritual.

To return to the early philosophers, who were mostly materialists, the record of their speculations is an interesting chapter in the history of rationalism. Two great names may be selected, Heraclitus and Democritus, because they did more perhaps than any of the others, by sheer hard thinking, to train reason to look

upon the universe in new ways and to shock the un-
reasoned conceptions of common sense. It was start-
ling to be taught, for the first time, by Heraclitus, that
the appearance of stability and permanence which
material things present to our senses is a false appearance, and that the world and everything in it are
changing every instant. Democritus performed the
amazing feat of working out an atomic theory of the
universe, which was revived in the seventeenth century
and is connected, in the history of speculation, with
the most modern physical and chemical theories of
matter. No fantastic tales of creation, imposed by sacred
authority, hampered these powerful brains.

All this philosophical speculation prepared the way
for the educationalists who were known as the Sophists.
They begin to appear after the middle of the fifth
century. They worked here and there throughout
Greece, constantly travelling, training young men for
public life, and teaching them to use their reason. As
educators they had practical ends in view. They
turned away from the problems of the physical universe
to the problems of human life—morality and politics.
Here they were confronted with the difficulty of distinguishing between truth and error, and the ablest of
them investigated the nature of knowledge, the method
of reason—logic—and the instrument of reason—
speech. Whatever their particular theories might be,
their general spirit was that of free inquiry and discussion. They sought to test everything by reason. The
second half of the fifth century might be called the age
of Illumination.

It may be remarked that the knowledge of foreign countries which the Greeks had acquired had a considerable effect in promoting a sceptical attitude towards authority. When a man is acquainted only with the habits of his own country, they seem so much a matter of course that he ascribes them to nature, but when he travels abroad and finds totally different habits and standards of conduct prevailing, he begins to understand the power of custom; and learns that morality and religion are matters of latitude. This discovery tends to weaken authority, and to raise disquieting reflections, as in the case of one who, brought up as a Christian, comes to realize that, if he had been born on the Ganges or the Euphrates, he would have firmly believed in entirely different dogmas.

Of course these movements of intellectual freedom were, as in all ages, confined to the minority. Everywhere the masses were exceedingly superstitious. They believed that the safety of their cities depended on the goodwill of their gods. If this superstitious spirit were alarmed, there was always a danger that philosophical speculations might be persecuted. And this occurred in Athens. About the middle of the fifth century Athens had not only become the most powerful State in Greece, but was also taking the highest place in literature and art. She was a full-fledged democracy. Political discussion was perfectly free. At this time she was guided by the statesman Pericles, who was personally a freethinker, or at least was in touch with all the subversive speculations of the day. He was especially intimate with the philosopher Anaxagoras who had come from Ionia

to teach at Athens. In regard to the popular gods
Anaxagoras was a thoroughgoing unbeliever. The
political enemies of Pericles struck at him by attacking
his friend. They introduced and carried a blasphemy
law, to the effect that unbelievers and those who taught
theories about the celestial world might be impeached.
It was easy to prove that Anaxagoras was a blasphemer
who taught that the gods were abstractions and that
the sun, to which the ordinary Athenian said prayers
morning and evening, was a mass of flaming matter.
The influence of Pericles saved him from death; he
was heavily fined and left Athens for Lampsacus,
where he was treated with consideration and honour.

Other cases are recorded which show that anti-
religious thought was liable to be persecuted. Protagoras, one of the greatest of the Sophists, published
a book *On the Gods*, the object of which seems to have
been to prove that one cannot know the gods by reason.
The first words ran: 'Concerning the gods, I cannot
say that they exist nor yet that they do not exist.
There are more reasons than one why we cannot know.
There is the obscurity of the subject and there is the
brevity of human life.' A charge of blasphemy was
lodged against him and he fled from Athens. But there
was no systematic policy of suppressing free thought.
Copies of the work of Protagoras were collected and
burned, but the book of Anaxagoras setting forth the
views for which he had been condemned was for sale
on the Athenian book-stalls at a popular price.
Rationalistic ideas moreover were venturing to appear
on the stage, though the dramatic performances, at

the feasts of the god Dionysus, were religious solemnities. The poet Euripides was saturated with modern speculation, and, while different opinions may be held as to the tendencies of some of his tragedies, he often allows his characters to express highly unorthodox views. He was prosecuted for impiety by a popular politician. We may suspect that during the last thirty years of the fifth century unorthodoxy spread considerably among the educated classes. There was a large enough section of influential rationalists to render impossible any organized repression of liberty, and the chief evil of the blasphemy law was that it could be used for personal or party reasons. Some of the prosecutions, about which we know, were certainly due to such motives, others may have been prompted by genuine bigotry and by the fear lest sceptical thought should extend beyond the highly educated and leisured class. It was a generally accepted principle among the Greeks, and afterwards among the Romans, that religion was a good and necessary thing for the common people. Men who did not believe in its truth believed in its usefulness as a political institution, and as a rule philosophers did not seek to diffuse disturbing 'truth' among the masses. It was the custom, much more than at the present day, for those who did not believe in the established cults to conform to them externally. Popular higher education was not an article in the programme of Greek statesmen or thinkers. And perhaps it may be argued that in the circumstances of the ancient world it would have been hardly practicable.

There was, however, one illustrious Athenian, who thought differently—Socrates, the philosopher. Socrates was the greatest of the educationalists, but unlike the others he taught gratuitously, though he was a poor man. His teaching always took the form of discussion; the discussion often ended in no positive result, but had the effect of showing that some received opinion was untenable and that truth is difficult to ascertain. He had indeed certain definite views about knowledge and virtue, which are of the highest importance in the history of philosophy, but for our present purpose his significance lies in his enthusiasm for discussion and criticism. He taught those with whom he conversed— and he conversed indiscriminately with all who would listen to him—to bring all popular beliefs before the bar of reason, to approach every inquiry with an open mind, and not to judge by the opinion of majorities or the dictate of authority; in short to seek for other tests of the truth of an opinion than the fact that it is held by a great many people. Among his disciples were all the young men who were to become the leading philosophers of the next generation and some who played prominent parts in Athenian history.

If the Athenians had had a daily press, Socrates would have been denounced by the journalists as a dangerous person. They had a comic drama, which constantly held up to ridicule philosophers and sophists and their vain doctrines. We possess one play (the *Clouds* of Aristophanes) in which Socrates is pilloried as a typical representative of impious and destructive speculations. Apart from annoyances of this kind,

Socrates reached old age, pursuing the task of instruct-
ing his fellow-citizens, without any evil befalling him.
Then, at the age of seventy, he was prosecuted as an
atheist and corrupter of youth and was put to death
(399 B.C.). It is strange that if the Athenians really
thought him dangerous they should have suffered him
so long. There can, I think, be little doubt that the
motives of the accusation were political.[1] Socrates,
looking at things as he did, could not be sympathetic
with unlimited democracy, or approve of the principle
that the will of the ignorant majority was a good guide.
He was probably known to sympathize with those who
wished to limit the franchise. When, after a struggle in
which the constitution had been more than once overthrown, democracy emerged triumphant (403 B.C.),
there was a bitter feeling against those who had not
been its friends, and of these disloyal persons Socrates
was chosen as a victim. If he had wished, he could
easily have escaped. If he had given an undertaking
to teach no more, he would almost certainly have been
acquitted. As it was, of the 501 ordinary Athenians
who were his judges, a very large minority voted for his
acquittal. Even then, if he had adopted a different tone,
he would not have been condemned to death.

He rose to the great occasion and vindicated freedom
of discussion in a wonderful unconventional speech. The
Apology of Socrates, which was composed by his most
brilliant pupil, Plato the philosopher, reproduces the

[1]This has been shown very clearly by Professor Jackson
in the article on 'Socrates' in the *Encyclopaedia Britannica*,
11th edition.

general tenor of his defence. It is clear that he was not able to meet satisfactorily the charge that he did not acknowledge the gods worshipped by the city, and his explanations on this point are the weak part of his speech. But he met the accusation that he corrupted the minds of the young by a splendid plea for free discussion. This is the most valuable section of the *Apology*; it is as impressive to-day as ever. I think the two principal points which he makes are these:

(1) He maintains that the individual should at any cost refuse to be coerced by any human authority or tribunal into a course which his own mind condemns as wrong. That is, he asserts *the supremacy of the individual conscience*, as we should say, over human law. He represents his own life-work as a sort of religious quest; he feels convinced that in devoting himself to philosophical discussion he has done the bidding of a superhuman guide; and he goes to death rather than be untrue to this personal conviction. 'If you propose to acquit me,' he says, 'on condition that I abandon my search for truth, I will say: I thank you, O Athenians, but I will obey God, who, as I believe, set me this task, rather than you, and so long as I have breath and strength I will never cease from my occupation with philosophy. I will continue the practice of accosting whomever I meet and saying to him, "Are you not ashamed of setting your heart on wealth and honours while you have no care for wisdom and truth and making your soul better?" I know not what death is— it may be a good thing, and I am not afraid of it. But

I do know that it is a bad thing to desert one's post and I prefer what may be good to what I know to be bad.'

(2) He insists on *the public value of free discussion.* 'In me you have a stimulating critic, persistently urging you with persuasion and reproaches, persistently testing your opinions and trying to show you that you are really ignorant of what you suppose you know. Daily discussion of the matters about which you hear me conversing is the highest good for man. Life that is not tested by such discussion is not worth living.'

Thus in what we may call the earliest justification of liberty of thought we have two significant claims affirmed: the indefeasible right of the conscience of the individual—a claim on which later struggles for liberty were to turn; and the social importance of discussion and criticism. The former claim is not based on argument but on intuition; it rests in fact on the assumption of some sort of superhuman moral principle, and to those who, not having the same personal experience as Socrates, reject this assumption, his pleading does not carry weight. The second claim, after the experience of more than 2,000 years, can be formulated more comprehensively now with bearings of which he did not dream.

The circumstances of the trial of Socrates illustrate both the tolerance and the intolerance which prevailed at Athens. His long immunity, the fact that he was at last indicted from political motives and perhaps personal also, the large minority in his favour, all show that thought was normally free, and that the mass of intolerance which existed was only fitfully invoked, and perhaps most often to serve other purposes. I may mention the case of the philosopher Aristotle, who some seventy years later left Athens because he was menaced by a prosecution for blasphemy, the charge being a pretext for attacking one who belonged to a certain political party. The persecution of opinion was never organized.

It may seem curious that to find the persecuting spirit in Greece we have to turn to the philosophers. Plato, the most brilliant disciple of Socrates, constructed in his later years an ideal State. In this State he instituted a religion considerably different from the current religion, and proposed to compel all the citizens to believe in his gods on pain of death or imprisonment. All freedom of discussion was excluded under the cast-iron system which he conceived. But the point of interest in his attitude is that he did not care much whether a religion was true, but only whether it was morally useful; he was prepared to promote morality by edifying fables; and he condemned the popular mythology not because it was false, but because it did not make for righteousness.

The outcome of the large freedom permitted at Athens was a series of philosophies which had a common source in the conversations of Socrates. Plato, Aristotle, the Stoics, the Epicureans, the Sceptics —it may be maintained that the efforts of thought represented by these names have had a deeper influence on the progress of man than any other continuous intellectual movement, at least until the rise of modern science in a new epoch of liberty.

The doctrines of the Epicureans, Stoics, and Sceptics all aimed at securing peace and guidance for the individual soul. They were widely propagated throughout the Greek world from the third century B.C., and we may say that from this time onward most well-educated Greeks were more or less rationalists. The teaching of Epicurus had a distinct anti-religious tendency. He considered fear to be the fundamental motive of religion, and to free men's minds from this fear was a principal object of his teaching. He was a materialist, explaining the world by the atomic theory of Democritus and denying any divine government of the universe. He did indeed hold the existence of gods, but, so far as men are concerned, his gods are as if they were not—living in some remote abode and enjoying a 'sacred and everlasting calm'. They just served as an example of the realization of the ideal Epicurean life.

There was something in this philosophy which had the power to inspire a poet of singular genius to expound it in verse. The Roman Lucretius (first century B.C.) regarded Epicurus as the great deliverer of the human race and determined to proclaim the glad tidings of his philosophy in a poem *On the Nature of the World*.[1] With all the fervour of a religious enthusiast he denounces religion, sounding every note of defiance, loathing, and contempt, and branding in burning words

[1] An admirable appreciation of the poem will be found in R. Y. Tyrrell's *Lectures on Latin Poetry*.

the crimes to which it had urged man on. He rides
forth as a leader of the hosts of atheism against the
walls of heaven. He explains the scientific arguments
as if they were the radiant revelation of a new world;
and the rapture of his enthusiasm is a strange accompaniment of a doctrine which aimed at perfect calm.
Although the Greek thinkers had done all the work and
the Latin poem is a hymn of triumph over prostrate
deities, yet in the literature of free thought it must
always hold an eminent place by the sincerity of its
audacious, defiant spirit. In the history of rationalism its
interest would be greater if it had exploded in the
midst of an orthodox community. But the educated
Romans in the days of Lucretius were sceptical in
religious matters, some of them were Epicureans, and
we may suspect that not many of those who read it
were shocked or influenced by the audacities of the
champion of irreligion.

The Stoic philosophy made notable contributions
to the cause of liberty and could hardly have flourished
in an atmosphere where discussion was not free. It
asserted the rights of individuals against public
authority. Socrates had seen that laws may be unjust
and that peoples may go wrong, but he had found no
principle for the guidance of society. The Stoics
discovered it in the law of nature, prior and superior
to all the customs and written laws of peoples, and this
doctrine, spreading outside Stoic circles, caught hold
of the Roman world and affected Roman legislation.

These philosophies have carried us from Greece to
Rome. In the later Roman Republic and the early

Empire, no restrictions were imposed on opinion,[1] and these philosophies, which made the individual the first consideration, spread widely. Most of the leading men were unbelievers in the official religion of the State, but they considered it valuable for the purpose of keeping the uneducated populace in order. A Greek historian expresses high approval of the Roman policy of cultivating superstition for the benefit of the masses. This was the attitude of Cicero, and the view that a false religion is indispensable as a social machine was general among ancient unbelievers. It is common, in one form or another to-day; at least, religions are constantly defended on the ground not of truth but of utility. This defence belongs to the statecraft of Machiavelli, who taught that religion is necessary for government, and that it may be the duty of a ruler to support a religion which he believes to be false.

A word must be said of Lucian (second century A.D.), the last Greek man of letters whose writings appeal to everybody. He attacked the popular mythology with open ridicule. It is impossible to say whether his satires had any effect at the time beyond affording enjoyment to educated infidels who read them. *Zeus in a Tragedy Part* is one of the most effective. The situation which Lucian imagined here would be paralleled if a modern writer were blasphemously to represent the Persons of the Trinity with some eminent

[1]Although opinion was free in Imperial Rome, writers were not protected from the retaliatory strokes of arbitrary power whenever susceptibilities were touched. For example: Tacitus, *Annals* IV, 34, VI, 39, XIV, 50; Suetonius, *Augustus* 31, *Tiberius* 61.—H.J.B.

angels and saints discussing in a celestial smoke-room
the alarming growth of unbelief in England and then
by means of a telephonic apparatus overhearing a
dispute between a freethinker and a parson on a public
platform in London. The absurdities of anthropo-
morphism have never been the subject of more brilliant
jesting than in Lucian's satires.

The general rule of Roman policy was to tolerate
throughout the Empire all religions and all opinions.
Blasphemy was not punished. The principle was
expressed in the maxim of the Emperor Tiberius:
'If the gods are insulted, let them see to it themselves.'
An exception to the rule of tolerance was made in the
case of the Christian sect, and the treatment of this
Oriental religion may be said to have inaugurated
religious persecution in Europe. It is a matter of
interest to understand why Emperors who were able,
humane, and not in the least fanatical, adopted this
exceptional policy.

For a long time the Christians were only known to
those Romans who happened to hear of them, as a
sect of the Jews. The Jewish was the one religion which,
on account of its exclusiveness and intolerance, was
regarded by the tolerant pagans with disfavour and
suspicion. But though it sometimes came into collision
with the Roman authorities and some ill-advised attacks
upon it were made, it was the constant policy of the
Emperors to let it alone and to protect the Jews against
the hatred which their own fanaticism aroused. But
while the Jewish religion was endured so long as it
was confined to those who were born into it, the

prospect of its dissemination raised a new question. Grave misgivings might arise in the mind of a ruler at seeing a creed spreading which was aggressively hostile to all the other creeds of the world—creeds which lived together in amity—and had earned for its adherents the reputation of being the enemies of the human race. Might not its expansion beyond the Israelites involve ultimately a danger to the Empire? For its spirit was incompatible with the traditions and basis of Roman society. The Emperor Domitian seems to have seen the question in this light, and he took severe measures to hinder the proselytizing of Roman citizens. Some of those whom he struck may have been Christians, but if he was aware of the distinction, there was from his point of view no difference. Christianity resembled Judaism, from which it sprang, in intolerance and in hostility towards Roman society, but it differed by the fact that it made many proselytes while Judaism made few.

Under Trajan we find that the principle has been laid down that to be a Christian is an offence punishable by death. Henceforward Christianity remained an illegal religion. But in practice the law was not applied rigorously or logically. The Emperors desired, if possible, to extirpate Christianity without shedding blood. Trajan laid down that Christians were not to be sought out, that no anonymous charges were to be noticed, and that an informer who failed to make good his charge should be liable to be punished under the laws against calumny. Christians themselves recognized that this edict practically protected them. There were some executions in the second century—not many that are well attested—and Christians courted the pain and glory of martyrdom. There is evidence to show that when they were arrested their escape was often connived at. In general, the persecution of the Christians was rather provoked by the populace than desired by the authorities. The populace felt a horror of this mysterious Oriental sect which openly hated all the gods and prayed for the destruction of the world. When floods, famines, and especially fires occurred they were apt to be attributed to the black magic of the Christians.

When any one was accused of Christianity, he was required, as a means of testing the truth of the charge, to offer incense to the gods or to the statues of deified emperors. His compliance at once exonerated him. The objection of the Christians—they and the Jews were the only objectors—to the worship of the emperors was, in the eyes of the Romans, one of the most sinister signs that their religion was dangerous. The purpose of this worship was to symbolize the unity and solidarity of an empire which embraced so many peoples of different beliefs and different gods; its intention was political, to promote union and loyalty; and it is not surprising that those who denounced it should be suspected of a disloyal spirit. But it must be noted that there was no necessity for any citizen to take part in this worship. No conformity was required from any inhabitants of the empire who were not serving the State as soldiers or civil functionaries. Thus the effect was to debar Christians from military and official careers.

The Apologies for Christianity which appeared at this period (second century) might have helped, if the Emperors (to whom some of them were addressed) had read them, to confirm the view that it was a political danger. It would have been easy to read between the lines that, if the Christians ever got the upper hand, they would not spare the cults of the State. The contemporary work of Tatian (*A Discourse to the Greeks*) reveals what the Apologists more or less sought to disguise, invincible hatred towards the civilization in which they lived. Any reader of the Christian literature of the time could not fail to see that in a State where Christians had the power there would be no tolerance of other religious practices.[1] If the Emperors made an exception to their tolerant policy in the case of Christianity, their purpose was to safeguard tolerance.

In the third century the religion, though still forbidden, was quite openly tolerated; the Church organized itself without concealment; ecclesiastical councils assembled without interference. There were some brief and local attempts at repression, there was only one grave persecution (begun by Decius, A.D. 250, and continued by Valerian). In fact, throughout this century, there were not many victims, though afterwards the Christians invented a whole mythology of martyrdoms. Many cruelties were imputed to emperors under whom we know that the Church enjoyed perfect peace.

[1]For the evidence of the Apologists see A. Bouché-Leclercq, *Religious Intolerance and Politics* (French, 1911)— a valuable review of the whole subject.

A long period of civil confusion, in which The Empire seemed to be tottering to its fall, had been terminated by the Emperor Diocletian, who, by his radical administrative reforms, helped to preserve the Roman power in its integrity for another century. He desired to support his work of political consolidation by reviving the Roman spirit, and he attempted to infuse new life into the official religion. To this end he determined to suppress the growing influence of the Christians, who, though a minority, were very numerous, and he organized a persecution. It was long, cruel and bloody; it was the most whole-hearted, general and systematic effort to crush the forbidden faith. It was a failure, the Christians were now too numerous to be crushed. After the abdication of Diocletian, the emperors who reigned in different parts of the realm did not agree as to the expediency of his policy, and the persecution ended by edicts of toleration (A.D. 311 and 313). These documents have an interest for the history of religious liberty.

The first, issued in the eastern provinces, ran as follows:

'We were particularly desirous of reclaiming into the way of reason and nature the deluded Christians, who had renounced the religion and ceremonies instituted by their fathers and, presumptuously despising the practice of antiquity, had invented extravagant laws and opinions according to the dictates of their fancy, and had collected a various society from the different provinces of our Empire. The edicts which we have published to enforce the worship of the gods, having exposed many of the Christians to danger and distress, many having suffered death and many more, who still persist in their impious folly, being left destitute of *any* public exercise of religion, we are disposed to extend to those unhappy men the effects of our wonted clemency. We permit them, therefore, freely to profess their private opinions, and to assemble in their conventicles without fear or molestation, provided always that they preserve a due respect to the established laws and government.'[1]

The second, of which Constantine was the author, known as the Edict of Milan, was to a similar effect, and based toleration on the emperor's care for the peace and happiness of his subjects and on the hope of appeasing the Deity whose seat is in heaven.

The relations between the Roman government and the Christians raised the general question of persecution and freedom of conscience. A State, with an official religion, but perfectly tolerant of all creeds and cults, finds that a society had arisen in its midst which is uncompromisingly hostile to all creeds but its own and which, if it had the power, would suppress all but its own. The government, in self-defence, decides to check the dissemination of these subversive ideas and makes the profession of that creed a crime, not on account of its particular tenets, but on account of the social consequences of those tenets. The members of the society cannot without violating their consciences and incurring damnation abandon their exclusive doctrine. The principle of freedom of conscience is asserted

[1]This is Gibbon's translation.

as superior to all obligations to the State, and the State, confronted by this new claim, is unable to admit it. Persecution is the result.

Even from the standpoint of an orthodox and loyal pagan the persecution of the Christians is indefensible, because blood was shed uselessly. In other words, it was a great mistake because it was unsuccessful. For persecution is a choice between two evils. The alternatives are violence (which no reasonable defender of persecution would deny to be an evil in itself) and the spread of dangerous opinions. The first is chosen simply to avoid the second, on the ground that the second is the greater evil. But if the persecution is not so devised and carried out as to accomplish its end, then you have two evils instead of one, and nothing can justify this. From their point of view, the Emperors had good reasons for regarding Christianity as dangerous and anti-social, but they should either have let it alone or taken systematic measures to destroy it. If at an early stage they had established a drastic and systematic inquisition, they might possibly have exterminated it. This at least would have been statesmanlike. But they had no conception of extreme measures, and they did not understand—they had no experience to guide them—the sort of problem they had to deal with. They hoped to succeed by intimidation. Their attempts at suppression were vacillating, fitful, and ridiculously ineffectual. The later persecutions (of A.D. 250 and 303) had no prospect of success. It is particularly to be observed that no effort was made to suppress Christian literature.

The higher problem whether persecution, even if it attains the desired end, is justifiable, was not considered. The struggle hinged on antagonism between the conscience of the individual and the authority and supposed interests of the State. It was the question which had been raised by Socrates, raised now on a wider platform in a more pressing and formidable shape: what is to happen when obedience to the law is inconsistent with obedience to an invisible master? Is it incumbent on the State to respect the conscience of the individual at all costs, or within what limits? The Christians did not attempt a solution, the general problem did not interest them. They claimed the right of freedom exclusively for themselves from a non-Christian government; and it is hardly going too far to suspect that they would have applauded the government if it had suppressed the Gnostic sects whom they hated and calumniated. In any case, when a Christian State was established, they would completely forget the principle which they had invoked. The martyrs died for conscience but not for liberty. To-day the greatest of the Churches demands freedom of conscience in the modern States which she does not control, but refuses to admit that, where she had the power, it would be incumbent on her to concede it.

If we review the history of classical antiquity as a whole, we may almost say that freedom of thought was like the air men breathed. It was taken for granted and nobody thought about it. If seven or eight thinkers at Athens were penalized for heterodoxy, in some and perhaps in most of these cases heterodoxy was only a pretext. They do not invalidate the general facts that the advance of knowledge was not impeded by prejudice, or science retarded by the weight of unscientific authority. The educated Greeks were tolerant because they were friends of reason and did not set up any authority to overrule reason. Opinions were not imposed except by argument; you were not expected to receive some 'kingdom of heaven' like a little child, or to prostrate your intellect before an authority claiming to be infallible.

But this liberty was not the result of a conscious policy or deliberate conviction, and therefore it was precarious. The problems of freedom of thought, religious liberty, toleration, had not been forced upon society and were never seriously considered. When Christianity confronted the Roman government, no one saw that in the treatment of a small, obscure, and, to pagan thinkers, uninteresting or repugnant sect, a principle of the deepest social importance was involved. A long experience of the theory and practice of persecution was required to base securely the theory of freedom of thought. The lurid policy of coercion which the Christian Church adopted, and its consequences, would at last compel reason to wrestle with the problem and discover the justification of intellectual liberty. The spirit of the Greeks and Romans, alive in their works, would, after a long period of obscuration, again enlighten the world and aid in re-establishing the reign of reason, which they had carelessly enjoyed without assuring its foundations.

Chapter III

REASON IN PRISON: THE MIDDLE AGES

ABOUT ten years after the Edict of Toleration, Constantine the Great adopted Christianity. This momentous decision inaugurated a millennium in which reason was enchained, thought was enslaved, and knowledge made no progress.

During the two centuries in which they had been a forbidden sect the Christians had claimed toleration on the ground that religious belief is voluntary and not a thing which can be enforced. When their faith became the predominant creed and had the power of the State behind it, they abandoned this view. They embarked on the hopeful enterprise of bringing about a complete uniformity in men's opinions on the mysteries of the universe, and began a more or less definite policy of coercing thought. This policy was adopted by emperors and governments partly on political grounds; religious divisions, bitter as they were, seemed dangerous to the unity of the State. But the fundamental principle lay in the doctrine that salvation is to be found exclusively in the Christian Church. The profound conviction that those who did not believe in its doctrines would be damned eternally, and that God punishes theological error as if it were the most heinous of crimes, led naturally to persecution. It was a duty to impose on men the only true doctrine, seeing that their own eternal interests were at stake, and to hinder errors from spreading. Heretics were more than ordinary criminals and the pains that man could inflict on them were as nothing to the tortures awaiting them in hell. To rid the earth of men who, however virtuous, were, through their religious errors, enemies of the Almighty, was a plain duty. Their virtues were no excuse. We must remember that, according to the humane doctrine of the Christians, pagan, that is, merely human, virtues were vices, and infants who died unbaptized passed the rest of time in creeping on the floor of hell. The intolerance arising from such views could not but differ in kind and intensity from anything that the world had yet witnessed.

Besides the logic of its doctrines, the character of its Sacred Book must also be held partly accountable for the intolerant principles of the Christian Church. It was unfortunate that the early Christians had included in their Scripture the Jewish writings which reflect the ideas of a low stage of civilization and are full of savagery. It would be difficult to say how much harm has been done, in corrupting the morals of men, by the precepts and examples of inhumanity, violence, and bigotry which the reverent reader of the Old Testament, implicitly believing in its inspiration, is bound to approve. It furnished an armoury for the theory of persecution. The truth is that Sacred Books are an obstacle to moral and intellectual progress, because they consecrate the ideas of a given epoch, and its customs, as divinely appointed. Christianity, by adopting books of a long past age, placed in the path of human development a particularly nasty stumbling block. It may occur to one to wonder how history might have been altered—altered it surely would have been—if the Christians had cut Jehovah out of their programme and, content with the New Testament, had rejected the inspiration of the Old.

Under Constantine the Great and his successors, edict after edict fulminated against the worship of the old pagan gods and against heretical Christian sects. Julian the Apostate, who in his brief reign (A.D. 361-3) sought to revive the old order of things, proclaimed universal toleration, but he placed Christians at a disadvantage by forbidding them to teach in schools. This was only a momentary check. Paganism was finally shattered by the severe laws of Theodosius I (end of fourth century). It lingered on here and there for more than another century, especially at Rome and Athens, but had little importance. The Christians were more concerned in striving among themselves than in crushing the prostrate spirit of antiquity. The execution of the heretic Priscillian in Spain (fourth century) inaugurated the punishment of heresy by death. It is interesting to see a non-Christian of this age teaching the Christian sects that they should suffer one another. Themistius in an address to the Emperor Valens urged him to repeal his edicts against the Christians with whom he did not agree, and expounded a theory of toleration. 'The religious beliefs of individuals are a field in which the authority of a government cannot be effective; compliance can only lead to hypocritical professions. Every faith should be allowed; the civil government should govern orthodox and heterodox to the common good. God himself plainly shows that he wishes various forms of worship; there are many roads by which one can reach him.'

No father of the Church has been more esteemed or enjoyed higher authority than St. Augustine (died A.D. 430). He formulated the principle of persecution[1] for the guidance of future generations, basing it on the firm foundation of Scripture—on words used by Jesus Christ in one of his parables, 'Compel them to come in.' Till the end of the twelfth century the Church worked hard to suppress heterodoxies. There was much persecution, but it was not systematic. There is reason to think that in the pursuit of heresy the Church was mainly guided by considerations of its temporal interest, and was roused to severe action only when the spread of false doctrine threatened to reduce its revenues or seemed a menace to society. At the end of the twelfth century Innocent III became Pope and under him the Church of western Europe reached the height of its power. He and his immediate successors are responsible for imagining and beginning an organized movement to sweep heretics out of Christendom. Languedoc in south-western France was largely populated by heretics, whose opinions were considered particularly offensive, known as the Albigeois. They were the subjects of the Count of Toulouse, and were an industrious and respectable people. But the Church

[1] The early Fathers, including Augustine, did not approve of the death penalty for heresy. Till late in the twelfth century more than one influential school of thought in the church were opposed to the punishment of heterodoxy as a crime.— H.J.B.

got far too little money out of this anti-clerical population, and Innocent called upon the Count to extirpate
heresy from his dominion. As he would not obey, the
Pope announced a Crusade against the Albigeois, and
offered to all who would bear a hand the usual rewards
granted to crusaders, including absolution from all
their sins. A series of sanguinary wars followed in which
the Englishman, Simon de Montfort, took part. There
were wholesale burnings and hangings of men, women
and children. The resistance of the people was broken
down, though the heresy was not eradicated, and the
struggle ended in 1229 with the complete humiliation
of the Count of Toulouse. The important point of the
episode is this: the Church introduced into the public
law of Europe the new principle that a sovran held his
crown on the condition that he should extirpate heresy.
If he hesitated to persecute at the command of the
Pope, he must be coerced; his lands were forfeited;
and his dominions were thrown open to be seized by
any one whom the Church could induce to attack him.
The Popes thus established a theocratic system in
which all other interests were to be subordinated to
the grand duty of maintaining the purity of the faith.

But in order to root out heresy it was necessary to
discover it in its most secret retreats. The Albigeois
had been crushed, but the poison of their doctrine
was not yet destroyed. The organized system of search-
ing out heretics known as the Inquisition was founded
by Pope Gregory IX about A.D. 1233, and fully
established by a Bull of Innocent IV (A.D. 1252) which
regulated the machinery of persecution 'as an integral

part of the social edifice in every city and every State'. This powerful engine for the suppression of the freedom of men's religious opinions is unique in history.

The bishops were not equal to the new task undertaken by the Church, and in every ecclesiastical province suitable monks were selected and to them was delegated the authority of the Pope for discovering heretics. These inquisitors had unlimited authority, they were subject to no supervision and responsible to no man. It would not have been easy to establish this system but for the fact that contemporary secular rulers had inaugurated independently a merciless legislation against heresy. The Emperor Frederick II, who was himself undoubtedly a freethinker, made laws for his extensive dominions in Italy and Germany (between 1220 and 1235), enacting that all heretics should be outlawed, that those who did not recant should be burned, those who recanted should be imprisoned, but if they relapsed should be executed; that their property should be confiscated, their houses destroyed, and their children, to the second generation, ineligible to positions of emolument unless they had betrayed their father or some other heretic.

Frederick's legislation consecrated the stake as the proper punishment for heresy. This cruel form of death for that crime seems to have been first inflicted on heretics by a French king (1017). We must remember that in the Middle Ages, and much later, crimes of all kinds were punished with the utmost cruelty. In England in the reign of Henry VIII there is a case of poisoners being boiled to death. Heresy was the foulest of all crimes; and to prevail against it was to prevail against the legions of hell. The cruel enactments against heretics were strongly supported by the public opinion of the masses.

When the Inquisition was fully developed it covered western Christendom with a net from the meshes of which it was difficult for a heretic to escape. The inquisitors in the various kingdoms co-operated, and communicated information; there was 'a chain of tribunals throughout continental Europe'. England stood outside the system, but from the age of Henry iv and Henry v the government repressed heresy by the stake under a special statute (A.D. 1400; repealed 1533; revived under Mary; finally repealed in 1676).

In its task of imposing unity of belief the Inquisition was most successful in Spain. Here towards the end of the fifteenth century a system was instituted which had peculiarities of its own and was very jealous of Roman interference. One of the achievements of the Spanish Inquisition (which was not abolished till the nineteenth century) was to expel the Moriscos or converted Moors, who retained many of their old Mohammadan opinions and customs. It is also said to have eradicated Judaism and to have preserved the country from the zeal of Protestant missionaries. But it cannot be proved that it deserves the credit of having protected Spain against Protestantism, for it is quite possible that if the seeds of Protestant opinion had been sown they would, in any case, have fallen dead on an uncongenial soil. Freedom of thought however was entirely suppressed.

One of the most efficacious means for hunting down heresy was the 'Edict of Faith', which enlisted the people in the service of the Inquisition and required every man to be an informer. From time to time a certain district was visited and an edict issued commanding those who knew anything of any heresy to come forward and reveal it, under fearful penalties temporal and spiritual. In consequence, no one was free from the suspicion of his neighbours or even of his own family. 'No more ingenious device has been invented to subjugate a whole population, to paralyse its intellect and to reduce it to blind obedience. It elevated delation to the rank of high religious duty.'

The process employed in the trials of those accused of heresy in Spain rejected every reasonable means for the ascertainment of truth. The prisoner was assumed to be guilty, the burden of proving his innocence rested on him; his judge was virtually his prosecutor. All witnesses against him, however infamous, were admitted. The rules for allowing witnesses for the prosecution were lax; those for rejecting witnesses for the defence were rigid. Jews, Moriscos, and servants could give evidence against the prisoner but not for him, and the same rule applied to kinsmen to the fourth degree. The principle on which the Inquisition proceeded was that better a hundred innocent should suffer than one guilty person escape. Indulgences were granted to any one who contributed wood to the pile. But the tribunal of the Inquisition did not itself condemn to the stake, for the Church must not be guilty of the shedding of blood. The ecclesiastical judge pronounced the prisoner to be a heretic of whose conversion there was no hope, and handed him over ('relaxed' him was the official term) to the secular authority, asking and charging the magistrate 'to treat him benignantly and mercifully'. But this formal plea for mercy could not be entertained by the civil power; it had no choice but to inflict death; if it did otherwise, it was a promoter of heresy. All princes and officials, according to the canon law, must punish duly and promptly heretics handed over to them by the Inquisition, under pain of excommunication. It is to be noted that the number of deaths at the stake has been much over-estimated by popular imagination; but the sum of suffering caused by the methods of the system and the punishments that fell short of death can hardly be exaggerated.

The legal processes employed by the Church in these persecutions exercised a corrupting influence on the criminal jurisprudence of the Continent. Lea, the historian of the Inquisition, observes: 'Of all the curses which the Inquisition brought in its train, this perhaps was the greatest—that, until the closing years of the eighteenth century, throughout the greater part of Europe, the inquisitorial process, as developed for the destruction of heresy, became the customary method of dealing with all who were under any accusation.'

The Inquisitors who, as Gibbon says, 'defended nonsense by cruelties', are often regarded as monsters. It may be said for them and for the kings who did their will that they were not a bit worse than the priests and monarchs of primitive ages who sacrificed human beings to their deities. The Greek king, Agamemnon, who immolated his daughter Iphigenia to obtain favourable winds from the gods, was perhaps a most affectionate father, and the seer who advised him to do so may have been a man of high integrity. They acted according to their beliefs. And so in the Middle Ages and afterwards men of kindly temper and the purest zeal for morality were absolutely devoid of mercy where heresy was suspected. Hatred of heresy was a sort of infectious germ, generated by the doctrine of exclusive salvation.

It has been observed that this dogma also injured the sense of truth. As man's eternal fate was at stake, it seemed plainly legitimate or rather imperative to use any means to enforce the true belief—even falsehood and imposture. There was no scruple about the invention of miracles or any fictions that were edifying. A disinterested appreciation of truth will not begin to prevail till the seventeenth century.

While this principle, with the associated doctrines of sin, hell, and the last judgement, led to such consequences, there were other doctrines and implications in Christianity which, forming a solid rampart against the advance of knowledge,[1] blocked the paths of science

[1]The story is far more complicated than any generalization can indicate. The scholastic disputations despised by the humanists first broke the dominion of mediaeval Aristotelianism and opened the way to the new views which made the dawn of modern science; theology favoured geometrizing, which was a better clue than observation and experiment to the theoretical reconstruction of the universe; Aristotle rather than the Bible formed the solid rampart. See *The Origins of Modern Science* (1949) by Herbert Butterfield for a view informed by twentieth-century researches.—H.J.B.

in the Middle Ages, and obstructed its progress till
the latter half of the nineteenth century. In every
important field of scientific research, the ground was
occupied by false views which the Church declared to
be true on the infallible authority of the Bible. The
Jewish account of Creation and the Fall of Man,
inextricably bound up with the Christian theory of
Redemption, excluded from free inquiry geology,
zoology, and anthropology. The literal interpretation
of the Bible involved the truth that the sun revolves
round the earth. The Church condemned the theory of
the antipodes. One of the charges against Servetus
(who was burned in the sixteenth century; see below,
p. 60) was that he believed the statement of a Greek
geographer that Judea is a wretched barren country
in spite of the fact that the Bible describes it as a land
flowing with milk and honey. The Greek physician
Hippocrates had based the study of medicine and
disease on experience and methodical research. In
the Middle Ages men relapsed to the primitive notions
of a barbarous age. Bodily ailments were ascribed to
occult agencies—the malice of the Devil or the wrath
of God. St. Augustine said that the diseases of Christians were caused by demons, and Luther in the same
way attributed them to Satan. It was only logical
that supernatural remedies should be sought to coun-
teract the effects of supernatural causes. There was an
immense traffic in relics with miraculous virtues, and
this had the advantage of bringing in a large revenue
to the Church. Physicians were often exposed to
suspicions of sorcery and unbelief. Anatomy was

forbidden, partly perhaps on account of the doctrine of the resurrection of the body. The opposition of ecclesiastics to inoculation in the eighteenth century was a survival of the mediaeval view of disease. Chemistry (alchemy) was considered a diabolical art and in 1317 was condemned by the Pope. The long imprisonment of Roger Bacon (thirteenth century) who, while he professed zeal for orthodoxy, had an inconvenient instinct for scientific research, illustrates the mediaeval distrust of science.

It is possible that the knowledge of nature would have progressed little, even if this distrust of science on theological grounds had not prevailed. For Greek science had ceased to advance 500 years before Christianity became powerful. After about 200 B.C. no important discoveries were made. The explanation of this decay is not easy, but we may be sure that it is to be sought in the social conditions of the Greek and Roman world. And we may suspect that the social conditions of the Middle Ages would have proved unfavourable to the scientific spirit—the disinterested quest of facts—even if the controlling beliefs had not been hostile. We may suspect that the rebirth of science would in any case have been postponed till new social conditions, which began to appear in the thirteenth century (see next chapter), had reached a certain maturity. Theological prejudice may have injured knowledge principally by its survival after the Middle Ages had passed away. In other words, the harm done by Christian doctrines, in this respect, may lie less in the obscurantism of the dark interval between ancient and modern civilization, than in the obstructions which they offered when science had revived in spite of them and could no longer be crushed.

The firm belief in witchcraft, magic, and demons was inherited by the Middle Ages from antiquity, but it became far more lurid and made the world terrible. Men believed that they were surrounded by fiends watching for every opportunity to harm them, that pestilences, storms, eclipses, and famines were the work of the devil; but they believed as firmly that ecclesiastical rites were capable of coping with these enemies. Some of the early Christian emperors legislated against magic, but till the fourteenth century there was no systematic attempt to root out witchcraft. The fearful epidemic, known as the Black Death, which devastated Europe in that century, seems to have aggravated the haunting terror of the invisible world of demons. Trials for witchcraft multiplied, and for 300 years the discovery of witchcraft and the destruction of those who were accused of practising it, chiefly women, was a standing feature of European civilization. Both the theory and the persecution were supported by Holy Scripture. 'Thou shalt not suffer a witch to live' was the clear injunction of the highest authority. Pope Innocent VIII issued a Bull on the matter (1484) in which he asserted that plagues and storms are the work of witches, and the ablest minds believed in the reality of their devilish powers.

No story is more painful than the persecution of witches, and nowhere was it more atrocious than in

England and Scotland. I mention it because it was the direct result of theological doctrines, and because, as we shall see, it was rationalism which brought the long chapter of horrors to an end.

In the period, then, in which the Church exercised its greatest influence, reason was enchained in the prison which Christianity had built around the human mind. It was not indeed inactive, but its activity took the form of heresy; or, to pursue the metaphor, those who broke chains were unable for the most part to scale the walls of the prison; their freedom extended only so far as to arrive at beliefs, which, like orthodoxy itself, were based on Christian mythology. There were some exceptions to the rule. At the end of the twelfth century a stimulus from another world began to make itself felt. The philosophy of Aristotle became known to learned men in western Christendom; their teachers were Jews and Mohammadans. Among the Moham- madans there was a certain amount of free thought, provoked by their knowledge of ancient Greek specu- lation. The works of the freethinker Averroës (twelfth century) which were based on Aristotle's philosophy, propagated a small wave of rationalism in Christian countries. Averroës held the eternity of matter and denied the immortality of the soul; his general view may be described as pantheism. But he sought to avoid difficulties with the orthodox authorities of Islam by laying down the doctrine of *double truth*, that is the coexistence of two independent and contra- dictory truths, the one philosophical, and the other religious. This did not save him from being banished from the court of the Spanish caliph. In the University of Paris his teaching produced a school of freethinkers who held that the Creation, the resurrection of the body, and other essential dogmas, might be true from the standpoint of religion but are false from the standpoint of reason. To a plain mind this seems much as if one said that the doctrine of immortality is true on Sundays but not on week-days, or that the Apostles' Creed is false in the drawing-room and true in the kitchen. This dangerous movement was crushed, and the saving principle of double truth condemned, by Pope John XXI. The spread of Averroistic and similar speculations called forth the *Theology* of Thomas, of Aquino in South Italy (died 1274), a most subtle thinker, whose mind had a natural turn for scepticism. He enlisted Aristotle, hitherto the guide of infidelity, on the side of orthodoxy, and constructed an ingenious Christian philosophy which is still authoritative in the Roman Church. But Aristotle and reason are dangerous allies for faith, and the treatise of Thomas is perhaps more calculated to unsettle a believing mind by the doubts which it powerfully states than to quiet the scruples of a doubter by its solutions.

There must always have been some private and underground unbelief here and there, which did not lead to any serious consequences. The blasphemous statement that the world had been deceived by three impostors, Moses, Jesus, and Mohammad, was current in the thirteenth century. It was attributed to the freethinking Emperor Frederick II (died 1250), who has been described as 'the first modern man'. The same idea, in a milder form, was expressed in the story of the Three Rings which is at least as old. A Mohammadan ruler, desiring to extort money from a rich Jew, summoned him to his court and laid a snare for him. 'My friend,' he said, 'I have often heard it reported that thou art a very wise man. Tell me therefore which of the three religions, that of the Jews, that of the Mohammadans, and that of the Christians, thou believest to be the truest.' The Jew saw that a trap was laid for him and answered as follows: 'My lord, there was once a rich man who among his treasures had a ring of such great value that he wished to leave it as a perpetual heirloom to his successors. So he made a will that whichever of his sons should be found in possession of this ring after his death should be considered his heir. The son to whom he gave the ring acted in the same way as his father, and so the ring passed from hand to hand. At last it came into the possession of a man who had three sons whom he loved equally. Unable to make up his mind to which of them he should leave the ring, he promised it to each of them privately, and then in order to satisfy them all caused a goldsmith to make two other rings so closely resembling the true ring that he was unable to distinguish them himself. On his death-bed he gave each of them a ring, and each claimed to be his heir, but no one could prove his title because the rings were indistinguishable, and the suit at law lasts till this day. It is even so, my lord, with the three religions, given by God to the three peoples. They each think they have the true religion, but which of them really has it, is a question, like that of the rings, still undecided.' This sceptical story became famous in the eighteenth century, when the German poet, Lessing, built upon it his drama *Nathan the Sage*, which was intended to show the unreasonableness of intolerance.

Chapter IV

PROSPECT OF DELIVERANCE: THE RENAISSANCE AND THE REFORMATION

The intellectual and social movement which was to dispel the darkness of the Middle Ages and prepare the way for those who would ultimately deliver reason from her prison, began in Italy in the thirteenth century. The misty veil woven of credulity and infantile naïveté which had hung over men's souls and protected them from understanding either themselves or their relation to the world began to lift. The individual began to feel his separate individuality, to be conscious of his own value as a person apart from his race or country (as in the later ages of Greece and Rome); and the world around him began to emerge from the mists of mediaeval dreams. The change was due to the political and social conditions of the little Italian States, of which some were republics and others governed by tyrants.

To the human world, thus unveiling itself, the individual who sought to make it serve his purposes required a guide; and the guide was found in the ancient literature of Greece and Rome. Hence the whole transformation, which presently extended from Italy to northern Europe, is known as the Renaissance, or rebirth of classical antiquity. But the awakened interest in classical literature, while it coloured the character and stimulated the growth of the movement, supplying new ideals and suggesting new points of view, was only the form in which the change of spirit began to express itself in the fourteenth century. The change might conceivably have taken some other shape. Its true name is Humanism.

At the time men hardly felt that they were passing into a new age of civilization, nor did the culture of the Renaissance immediately produce any open or general intellectual rebellion against orthodox beliefs. The world was gradually assuming an aspect decidedly unfriendly to the teaching of mediaeval orthodoxy; but there was no explosion of hostility; it was not till the seventeenth century that war between religion and authority was systematically waged. The humanists were not hostile to theological authority or to the claims of religious dogma; but they had discovered a purely human curiosity about this world and it absorbed their interest. They idolized pagan literature which abounded in poisonous germs; the secular side of education became all-important; religion and theology were kept in a separate compartment. Some speculative minds, which were sensitive to the contradiction, might seek to reconcile the old religion with new ideas; but the general tendency of thinkers in the Renaissance period was to keep the two worlds distinct, and to practise outward conformity to the creed without any real intellectual submission.

I may illustrate this double-facedness of the Renaissance by Montaigne (second half of sixteenth century). His *Essays* make for rationalism but contain frequent professions of orthodox Catholicism, in which he was perfectly sincere. There is no attempt to reconcile the two points of view; in fact, he takes the sceptical position that there is no bridge between reason and religion. The human intellect is incapable in the domain of theology, and religion must be placed aloft, out of reach and beyond the interference of reason; to be humbly accepted. But while he humbly accepted it, on sceptical grounds which would have induced him to accept Mohammadanism if he had been born in Cairo, his soul was not in its dominion. It was the philosophers and wise men of antiquity, Cicero, and Seneca, and Plutarch, who moulded and possessed his mind. It is to them, and not to the consolations of Christianity, that he turns when he discusses the problem of death. The religious wars in France which he witnessed and the Massacre of St. Bartholomew's Day (1572) were calculated to confirm him in his scepticism. His attitude to persecution is expressed in the remark that 'it is setting a high value on one's opinions to roast men on account of them'.

The logical results of Montaigne's scepticism were made visible by his friend Charron, who published a book *On Wisdom* in 1601. Here it is taught that true morality is not founded on religion, and the author surveys the history of Christianity to show the evils which it had produced. He says of immortality that it is the most generally received doctrine, the most usefully believed, and the most weakly established by human reasons; but he modified this and some other passages in a second edition. A contemporary Jesuit placed Charron in the catalogue of the most dangerous and wicked atheists. He was really a deist; but in those days, and long after, no one scrupled to call a non-Christian deist an atheist. His book would doubtless have been suppressed and he would have suffered but for the support of King Henry IV. It has a particular interest because it transports us directly from the atmosphere of the Renaissance, represented by Montaigne, into the new age of more or less aggressive rationalism.

What Humanism did in the fourteenth, fifteenth and sixteenth centuries, at first in Italy, then in other countries, was to create an intellectual atmosphere in which the emancipation of reason could begin and knowledge could resume its progress. The period saw the invention of printing and the discovery of new parts of the globe, and these things were to aid powerfully in the future defeat of authority.

But the triumph of freedom depended on other causes also; it was not to be brought about by the intellect alone. The chief political facts of the period were the decline of the power of the Pope in Europe, the decay of the Holy Roman Empire, and the growth of strong monarchies, in which worldly interests determined and dictated ecclesiastical policy, and from which the modern State was to develop. The success of the Reformation was made possible by these conditions. Its victory in north Germany was due to the secular interest of the princes, who profited by the confiscation of Church lands. In England there was no popular movement; the change was carried through by the government for its own purposes.

The principal cause of the Reformation was the general corruption of the Church and the flagrancy of its oppression. For a long time the Papacy had had no higher aim than to be a secular power exploiting its spiritual authority for the purpose of promoting its worldly interests, by which it was exclusively governed. All the European States based their diplomacy on this assumption. Since the fourteenth century every one acknowledged the need of reforming the Church, and reform had been promised, but things went from bad to worse, and there was no resource but rebellion. The rebellion led by Luther was the result not of a revolt of reason against dogmas, but of widely spread anti-clerical feeling due to the ecclesiastical methods of extorting money, particularly by the sale of Indulgences, the most glaring abuse of the time. It was his study of the theory of Papal Indulgences that led Luther on to his theological heresies.[1]

It is an elementary error, but one which is still shared by many people who have read history superficially, that the Reformation established religious liberty and the right of private judgement. What it did

---

[1]Luther seems from the first to have been more interested in attacking the doctrine than the life, and says so. In the Leipzig debate with Eck, Indulgences are a minor issue, it is the foundation of the faith that is in question. 'I want to believe freely and be a slave to the authority of no one, whether council, university, or pope. I will confidently confess what appears to me to be true, whether it has been asserted by a Catholic or a heretic, whether it has been approved or reproved by a council.' R. Bainton, *Here I Stand*, p. 119. But Luther's revolt undoubtedly brought back fanatical religion into a corrupt and easy-going Church, and made it less favourable to secular interests.—H.J.B.

was to bring about a new set of political and social
conditions, under which religious liberty could ultimately be secured, and, by virtue of its inherent
inconsistencies, to lead to results at which its leaders
would have shuddered. But nothing was further from
the minds of the leading Reformers than the toleration
of doctrines differing from their own. They replaced
one authority by another. They set up the authority
of the Bible instead of that of the Church, but it was
the Bible according to Luther or the Bible according
to Calvin. So far as the spirit of intolerance went, there
was nothing to choose between the new and the old
Churches. The religious wars were not for the cause
of freedom, but for particular sets of doctrines; and
in France, if the Protestants had been victorious, it is
certain that they would not have given more liberal
terms to the Catholics than the Catholics gave to them.

Luther was quite opposed to liberty of conscience
and worship, a doctrine which was inconsistent with
Scripture as he read it. He might protest against
coercion and condemn the burning of heretics, when
he was in fear that he and his party might be victims,
but when he was safe and in power, he asserted his
real view that it was the duty of the State to impose the
true doctrine and exterminate heresy, which was an
abomination, that unlimited obedience to their prince
in religious as in other matters was the duty of subjects,
and that the end of the State was to defend the faith.
He held that Anabaptists should be put to the sword.
With Protestants and Catholics alike the dogma of
exclusive salvation led to the same place.

Calvin's fame for intolerance is blackest. He did not, like Luther, advocate the absolute power of the civil ruler; he stood for the control of the State by the Church—a form of government which is commonly called theocracy; and he established a theocracy at Geneva. Here liberty was completely crushed; false doctrines were put down by imprisonment, exile, and death. The punishment of Servetus is the most famous exploit of Calvin's warfare against heresy. The Spaniard Servetus, who had written against the dogma of the Trinity, was imprisoned at Lyons (partly through the machinations of Calvin) and having escaped came rashly to Geneva. He was tried for heresy and committed to the flames (1553), though Geneva had no jurisdiction over him. Melanchthon, who formulated the principles of persecution, praised this act as a memorable example to posterity. Posterity however was one day to be ashamed of that example. In 1903 the Calvinists of Geneva felt impelled to erect an expiatory monument, in which Calvin 'our great Reformer' is excused as guilty of an error 'which was that of his century'.

Thus the Reformers, like the Church from which they parted, cared nothing for freedom, they only cared for 'truth'. If the mediaeval ideal was to purge the world of heretics, the object of the Protestant was to exclude all dissidents from his own land. The people at large were to be driven into a fold, to accept their faith at the command of their sovran. This was the principle laid down in the religious peace which (1555) composed the struggle between the Catholic emperor and the Protestant German princes. It was recognized by Catherine de' Medici when she massacred the French Protestants and signified to Queen Elizabeth that *she* might do likewise with English Catholics.

Nor did the Protestant creeds represent enlightenment. The Reformation on the Continent was as hostile to enlightenment as it was to liberty; and science, if it seemed to contradict the Bible, had as little chance with Luther as with the Pope. The Bible, interpreted by the Protestants or the Roman Church, was equally fatal to witches. In Germany the development of learning received a long set-back.[1]

Yet the Reformation involuntarily helped the cause of liberty. The result was contrary to the intentions of its leaders, was indirect, and long delayed. In the first place, the great rent in western Christianity, substituting a number of theological authorities instead of one—several gods, we may say, instead of one God—produced a weakening of ecclesiastical authority in general. The religious tradition was broken. In the second place, in the Protestant States, the supreme ecclesiastical power was vested in the sovran; the sovran had other interests besides those of the Church to consider; and political reasons would compel him sooner or later to modify the principle of ecclesiastical

[1] It was humanism, said to have found in Germany a second home, which prepared the way for the Reformation and helped to disintegrate mediaeval scholasticism, and the supporters of Luther were the pupils of the humanists. But Reformation and Counter-reformation both meant a check to Renaissance interests. Between the neo-scholastic Protestants and the Catholic Jesuits there was little room for the spirit of Erasmus.—H.J.B.

intolerance. Catholic States in the same way were forced to depart from the duty of not suffering heretics. The religious wars in France ended in a limited toleration of Protestants. The policy of Cardinal Richelieu, who supported the Protestant cause in Germany, illustrates how secular interests obstructed the cause of faith.

Again, the intellectual justification of the Protestant rebellion against the Church had been the right of private judgement, that is, the principle of religious liberty. But the Reformers had asserted it only for themselves, and as soon as they had framed their own articles of faith, they had practically repudiated it. This was the most glaring inconsistency in the Protestant position; and the claim which they had thrust aside could not be permanently suppressed. Once more, the Protestant doctrines rested on an insecure foundation which no logic could defend, and inevitably led from one untenable position to another. If we are to believe on authority, why should we prefer the upstart dictation of the Lutheran Confession of Augsburg or the English Thirty-nine Articles to the venerable authority of the Church of Rome? If we decide against Rome, we must do so by means of reason; but once we exercise reason in the matter, why should we stop where Luther or Calvin or any of the other rebels stopped, unless we assume that one of them was inspired? If we reject superstitions which they rejected, there is nothing except *their* authority to prevent us from rejecting all or some of the superstitions which they retained. Moreover, their Bible-worship promoted results which they did not foresee.[1] The inspired record on which the creeds depend became an open book. Public attention was directed to it as never before, though it cannot be said to have been universally read before the nineteenth century. Study led to criticism, the difficulties of the dogma of inspiration were appreciated, and the Bible was ultimately to be submitted to a remorseless dissection which has altered at least the quality of its authority in the eyes of intelligent believers. This process of Biblical criticism has been conducted mainly in a Protestant atmosphere and the new position in which the Bible was placed by the Reformation must be held partly accountable. In these ways, Protestantism was adapted to be a stepping-stone to rationalism, and thus served the cause of freedom.

That cause however was powerfully and directly promoted by one sect of Reformers, who in the eyes of all the others were blasphemers and of whom most people never think when they talk of the Reformation. I mean the Socinians. Of their far-reaching influence something will be said in the next chapter.

Another result of the Reformation has still to be mentioned, its renovating effect on the Roman Church, which had now to fight for its existence. A new series of Popes who were in earnest about religion began with Paul III (1534) and reorganized the Papacy and its resources for a struggle of centuries.[2] The institution

[1] The danger, however, was felt in Germany, and in the seventeenth century the study of Scripture was not encouraged at German universities.

[2] See Barry, *Papacy and Modern Times*, 113 seq.

of the Jesuit order, the establishment of the Inquisition at Rome, the Council of Trent, the censorship of the Press (Index of Forbidden Books) were the expression of the new spirit and the means to cope with the new situation. The reformed Papacy was good fortune for believing children of the Church, but what here concerns us is that one of its chief objects was to repress freedom more effectually. Savonarola who preached right living at Florence had been executed (1498) under Pope Alexander VI who was a notorious profligate. If Savonarola had lived in the new era he might have been canonized, but Giordano Bruno was burned.

Giordano Bruno had constructed a religious philosophy, based partly upon Epicurus, from whom he took the theory of the infinity of the universe. But Epicurean materialism was transformed into a pantheistic mysticism by the doctrine that God is the soul of matter. Accepting the recent discovery of Copernicus, which Catholics and Protestants alike rejected, that the earth revolves round the sun, Bruno took the further step of regarding the fixed stars as suns, each with its invisible satellites. He sought to come to an understanding with the Bible, which (he held) being intended for the vulgar had to accommodate itself to their prejudices. Leaving Italy, because he was suspected of heresy, he lived successively in Switzerland, France, England, and Germany, and in 1592, induced by a false friend to return to Venice he was seized by order of the Inquisition. Finally condemned in Rome, he was burned (1600) in the Campo de' Fiori, where a

monument now stands in his honour, erected some
years ago, to the great chagrin of the Roman
church.

Much is made of the fate of Bruno because he is one
of the world's famous men. No country has so illustrious a victim of that era to commemorate as Italy,
but in other lands blood just as innocent was shed for
heterodox opinions. In France there was rather more
freedom than elsewhere under the relatively tolerant
government of Henry IV and of the Cardinals Richelieu
and Mazarin, till about 1660. But at Toulouse (1619)
Lucilio Vanini, a learned Italian who like Bruno
wandered about Europe, was convicted as an atheist
and blasphemer; his tongue was torn out and he was
burned. Protestant England, under Elizabeth and
James I, did not lag behind the Roman Inquisition,
but on account of the obscurity of the victims her zeal
for faith has been unduly forgotten. Yet, but for an
accident, she might have covered herself with the glory
of having done to death a heretic not less famous than
Giordano Bruno. The poet Marlowe was accused of
atheism, but while the prosecution was hanging over
him he was killed in a sordid quarrel in a tavern (1593).
Another dramatist (Kyd) who was implicated in the
charge was put to the torture. At the same time Sir
Walter Raleigh was prosecuted for unbelief but not
convicted. Others were not so fortunate. Three or four
persons were burned at Norwich in the reign of
Elizabeth for unchristian doctrines, among them
Francis Kett who had been a Fellow of Corpus
Christi, Cambridge. Under James I, who interested

himself personally in such matters, Bartholomew Legate was charged with holding various pestilent opinions. The king summoned him to his presence and asked him whether he did not pray daily to Jesus Christ. Legate replied he had prayed to Christ in the days of his ignorance, but not for the last seven years. 'Away, base fellow,' said James, spurning him with his foot, 'it shall never be said that one stayeth in my palace that hath never prayed to our Saviour for seven years together.' Legate, having been imprisoned for some time in Newgate, was declared an incorrigible heretic and burned at Smithfield (1611). Just a month later, one Wightman was burned at Lichfield, by the Bishop of Coventry, for heterodox doctrines. It is possible that public opinion was shocked by these two burnings. They were the last cases in England of death for unbelief. Puritan intolerance, indeed, passed an ordinance in 1648, by which all who denied the Trinity, Christ's divinity, the inspiration of Scripture, or a future state, were liable to death, and persons guilty of other heresies, to imprisonment. But this did not lead to any executions.

The Renaissance age saw the first signs of the beginning of modern science,[1] but the mediaeval prejudices against the investigation of nature were not dissipated till the seventeenth century, and in Italy

[1]The Renaissance did not initiate the development of modern science, it rediscovered ancient science. The initiative came rather from the scholastics. See Prof. Butterfield's reference to the work of Jean Buridan and Nicholas of Oresme in the mid-fourteenth century. *Origins of Modern Science*, p. 7.—H.J.B.

they continued to a much later period. The history of modern astronomy begins in 1543, with the publication of the work of Copernicus revealing the truth about the motions of the earth. The appearance of this work is important in the history of free thought, because it raised a clear and definite issue between science and Scripture; and Osiander, who edited it (Copernicus was dying), foreseeing the outcry it would raise, stated untruly in the preface that the earth's motion was put forward only as a hypothesis. The theory was denounced by Catholics and Reformers, and it did not convince some men (e.g. Bacon) who were not influenced by theological prejudice. The observations of the Italian astronomer Galileo de' Galilei demonstrated the Copernican theory beyond question. His telescope discovered the moons of Jupiter, and his observation of the spots in the sun confirmed the earth's rotation. In the pulpits of Florence, where he lived under the protection of the Grand Duke, his sensational discoveries were condemned. 'Men of *Galilee*, why stand ye gazing up into heaven?' He was then denounced to the Holy Office of the Inquisition by two Dominican monks. Learning that his investigations were being considered at Rome, Galileo went thither, confident that he would be able to convince the ecclesiastical authorities of the manifest truth of Copernicanism. He did not realize what theology was capable of. In February 1616 the Holy Office decided that the Copernican system was in itself absurd, and, in respect of Scripture, heretical. Cardinal Bellarmin, by the Pope's direction, summoned Galileo and officially admonished him to abandon his opinion and cease to teach it, otherwise the Inquisition would proceed against him. Galileo promised to obey. The book of Copernicus was placed on the Index. It has been remarked that Galileo's book on *Solar Spots* contains no mention of Scripture, and thus the Holy Office, in its decree which related to that book, passed judgement on a scientific, not a theological, question.

Galileo was silenced for a while, but it was impossible for him to be mute for ever. Under a new Pope (Urban VIII) he looked for greater liberty, and there were many in the Papal circle who were well disposed to him. He hoped to avoid difficulties by the device of placing the arguments for the old and the new theories side by side, and pretending not to judge between them. He wrote a treatise on the two systems (the Ptolemaic and the Copernican) in the form of *Dialogues*, of which the preface declares that the purpose is to explain the pros and cons of the two views. But the spirit of the work is Copernican. He received permission, quite definite as he thought, from Father Riccardi (master of the Sacred Palace) to print it, and it appeared in 1632. The Pope however disapproved of it, the book was examined by a commission, and Galileo was summoned before the Inquisition. He was old and ill, and the humiliations which he had to endure are a painful story. He would probably have been more severely treated, if one of the members of the tribunal had not been a man of scientific training (Macolano, a Dominican), who was able to appreciate his ability. Under examination, Galileo denied that he had upheld the motion of the earth in the *Dialogues*, and asserted that he had shown the reasons of Copernicus to be inconclusive. This defence was in accordance with the statement in his preface, but contradicted his deepest conviction. In struggling with such a tribunal, it was the only line which a man who was not a hero could take. At a later session, he forced himself ignominiously to confess that some of the arguments on the Copernican side had been put too strongly and to declare himself ready to confute the theory. In the final examination, he was threatened with torture. He said that before the decree of 1616 he had held the truth of the Copernican system to be arguable, but since then he had held the Ptolemaic to be true. Next day, he publicly abjured the scientific truth which he had demonstrated. He was allowed to retire to the country, on condition that he saw no one. In the last months of his life he wrote to a friend to this effect: 'The falsity of the Copernican system cannot be doubted, especially by us Catholics. It is refuted by the irrefragable authority of Scripture. The conjectures of Copernicus and his disciples were all disposed of by the one solid argument: God's omnipotence can operate in infinitely various ways. If something appears to our observation to happen in one particular way, we must not curtail God's arm, and sustain a thing in which we may be deceived.' The irony is evident.

Rome did not permit the truth about the solar system to be taught till after the middle of the eighteenth century, and Galileo's books remained on the Index till 1835. The prohibition embarrassed the study of natural science in Italy.

The Roman Index reminds us of the significance of the invention of printing in the struggle for freedom of thought, by making it easy to propagate new ideas, far and wide. Authority speedily realized the danger and took measures to place its yoke on the new contrivance, which promised to be such a powerful ally of reason. Pope Alexander VI inaugurated censorship of the press by his Bull against unlicensed printing (1501). In France, King Henry II made printing without official permission punishable by death. In Germany, censorship was introduced in 1529. In England, under Elizabeth, books could not be printed without a licence, and printing presses were not allowed except in London, Oxford, and Cambridge; the regulation of the press was under the authority of the Star Chamber. Nowhere did the press become really free till the nineteenth century.

While the Reformation and the renovated Roman Church meant a reaction against the Renaissance, the vital changes which the Renaissance signified—individualism, a new intellectual attitude to the world, the cultivation of secular knowledge—were permanent and destined to lead, amid the competing intolerances of Catholic and Protestant powers, to the goal of liberty. We shall see how reason and the growth of knowledge undermined the bases of theological authority. At each step in this process, in which philosophical speculation, historical criticism, natural science have all taken part, the opposition between reason and faith deepened; doubt, clear or vague, increased; and secularism, derived from the Humanists,[1] and always implying scepticism, whether latent or conscious, substituted an interest in the fortunes of the human race upon earth for the interest in a future world. And along with this steady intellectual advance, toleration gained ground and freedom won more champions. In the meantime the force of political circumstances was compelling governments to mitigate their maintenance of one religious creed by measures of relief to other Christian sects, and the principle of exclusiveness was broken down for reasons of worldly expediency. *Religious* liberty was an important step towards complete freedom of opinion.

[1]The university of Padua, more than any other, bred the men and developed the schools of thought which made the scientific revolution of the sixteenth and seventeenth centuries. It was under secular control and it was derided by the Humanists for its averroistic Aristotelianism: it responded by developing a new scientific humanism. See J. H. Randall, Jr.'s Introduction to Pomponazzi in *The Renaissance Philosophy of Man* (Chicago, 1948). — H.J.B.

Chapter V

RELIGIOUS TOLERATION

IN THE third century B.C. the Indian king Asoka, a man of religious zeal but of tolerant spirit, confronted by the struggle between two hostile religions (Brahmanism and Buddhism), decided that both should be equally privileged and honoured in his dominions. His ordinances on the matter are memorable as the earliest existing edicts of toleration. In Europe, as we saw, the principle of toleration was for the first time definitely expressed in the Roman imperial edicts which terminated the persecution of the Christians.

The religious strife of the sixteenth century raised the question in its modern form, and for many generations it was one of the chief problems of statesmen and the subject of endless controversial pamphlets. Toleration means incomplete religious liberty, and there are many degrees of it. It might be granted to certain Christian sects; it might be granted to Christian sects, but these alone; it might be granted to all religions, but not to freethinkers; or to deists, but not to atheists. It might mean the concession of some civil rights, but not of others; it might mean the exclusion of those who are tolerated from public offices or from certain professions. The religious liberty now enjoyed in western

lands has been gained through various stages of toleration.

We owe the modern principle of toleration to the
Italian group of reformers, who rejected the doctrine
of the Trinity and were the fathers of Unitarianism.
The Reformation movement had spread to Italy, but
Rome was successful in suppressing it, and many
heretics fled to Switzerland. The anti-Trinitarian group
were forced by the intolerance of Calvin to flee to
Transylvania and Poland where they propagated their
doctrines. The Unitarian creed was moulded by Fausto
Sozzini, generally known as Socinus, and in the
catechism of his sect (1574) persecution is condemned.
This repudiation of the use of force in the interest of
religion is a consequence of the Socinian doctrines.
For, unlike Luther and Calvin, the Socinians conceded
such a wide room to individual judgement in the
interpretation of Scripture that to impose Socinianism
would have been inconsistent with its principles. In
other words, there was a strong rationalistic element
which was lacking in the Trinitarian creeds.

It was under the influence of the Socinian spirit[1]
that Castellion of Savoy sounded the trumpet of

[1]Bury follows his friend Ruffini in tracing the idea and
practice of toleration to the Socinians, but this is an ana-
chronism in the case of Castellio who contributed to the
making of this spirit. He was influenced by Italian humanism
and neo-platonism, but the widespread influence of *Satanae
stratagematum libri octo* (1565), the work of his disciple
Acontius, gives him 'a strong claim to be considered as the
pioneer' in the assertion of the principle of freedom of
religious inquiry. See *Socinianism in Seventeenth-Century
England* by H. J. McLachlan (O.U.P., 1951), pp. 8 and
55–62.—H.J.B.

toleration in a pamphlet denouncing the burning of Servetus, whereby he earned the malignant hatred of Calvin. He maintained the innocence of error and ridiculed the importance which the Churches laid on obscure questions such as predestination and the Trinity. 'To discuss the difference between the Law and the Gospel, gratuitous remission of sins or imputed righteousness, is as if a man were to discuss whether a prince was to come on horseback, or in a chariot, or dressed in white or in red.'[1] Religion is a curse if persecution is a necessary part of it.

For a long time the Socinians and those who came under their influence when, driven from Poland, they passed into Germany and Holland, were the only sects which advocated toleration. It was adopted from them by the Anabaptists and by the Arminian section of the Reformed Church of Holland. And in Holland, the founder of the English Congregationalists, who (under the name of Independents) played such an important part in the history of the Civil War and the Commonwealth, learned the principle of liberty of conscience.

Socinus thought that this principle could be realized without abolishing the State Church. He contemplated a close union between the State and the prevailing Church, combined with complete toleration for other sects. It is under this system (which has been called *jurisdictional*) that religious liberty has been realized in European States. But there is another and simpler method, that of *separating* Church from State and

[1] Translated by Lecky.

placing all religions on an equality. This was the solution which the Anabaptists would have preferred. They detested the State; and the doctrine of religious liberty was not precious to them. Their ideal system would have been an Anabaptist theocracy; separation was the second best.

In Europe, public opinion was not ripe for separation, inasmuch as the most powerful religious bodies were alike in regarding toleration as wicked indifference. But it was introduced in a small corner of the new world beyond the Atlantic in the seventeenth century. The Puritans who fled from the intolerance of the English Church and State and founded colonies in New England, were themselves equally intolerant, not only to Anglicans and Catholics, but to Baptists and Quakers. They set up theocratical governments from which all who did not belong to their own sect were excluded. Roger Williams had imbibed from the Dutch Arminians the idea of separation of Church from State. On account of this heresy he was driven from Massachusetts, and he founded Providence to be a refuge for those whom the Puritan colonists persecuted. Here he set up a democratic constitution in which the magistrates had power only in civil matters and could not interfere with religion. Other towns were presently founded in Rhode Island, and a charter of Charles II (1663) confirmed the constitution, which secured to all citizens professing Christianity, of whatever form, the full enjoyment of political rights. Non-Christians were tolerated, but were not admitted to the political rights of Christians. So far, the new

State fell short of perfect liberty. But the fact that Jews were soon admitted, notwithstanding, to full citizenship shows how free the atmosphere was. To Roger Williams belongs the glory of having founded the first modern State which was really tolerant and was based on the principle of taking the control of religious matters entirely out of the hands of the civil government.

Toleration was also established in the Roman Catholic colony of Maryland, but in a different way. Through the influence of Lord Baltimore an Act of Toleration was passed in 1649, notable as the first decree, voted by a legal assembly, granting complete freedom to all Christians. No one professing faith in Christ was to be molested in regard to his religion. But the law was heavy on all outside this pale. Any one who blasphemed God or attacked the Trinity or any member of the Trinity was threatened by the penalty of death. The tolerance of Maryland attracted so many Protestant settlers from Virginia that the Protestants became a majority, and as soon as they won political preponderance, they introduced an Act (1654) excluding Papists and Prelatists from toleration. The rule of the Baltimores was restored after 1660, and the old religious freedom was revived, but with the accession of William III the Protestants again came into power and the toleration which the Catholics had instituted in Maryland came to an end.

It will be observed that in both these cases freedom was incomplete; but it was much larger and more fundamental in Rhode Island, where it had been ultimately derived from the doctrine of Socinus.[1] When the colonies became independent of England the federal constitution which they set up was absolutely secular, but it was left to each member of the Union to adopt Separation or not (1789). If separation has become the rule in the American States, it may be largely due to the fact that on any other system the governments would have found it difficult to impose mutual tolerance on the sects. It must be added that in Maryland and a few southern States atheists still suffer from some political disabilities.

In England, the experiment of separation would have been tried under the Commonwealth, if the Independents had had their way. This policy was overruled by Cromwell. The new national Church included Presbyterians, Independents, and Baptists, but liberty of worship was granted to all Christian sects, except Roman Catholics and Anglicans. If the parliament had had the power, this toleration would have been a mere name. The Presbyterians regarded toleration as a work of the devil, and would have persecuted the Independents if they could. But under Cromwell's autocratic rule even the Anglicans lived in peace, and toleration was extended to the Jews. In these days, voices were raised from various quarters advocating toleration on general grounds.[2] The

[1] Complete toleration was established by Penn in the Quaker Colony of Pennsylvania in 1682. [The principle of the separation of Church and State was based by Roger Williams on the fundamental cleavage between the elect and the non-elect, not upon the doctrines of Socinus.—H.J.B.]

[2] Especially Chillingworth's *Religion of Protestants* (1637), and Jeremy Taylor's *Liberty of Prophesying* (1646).

most illustrious advocate was Milton, the poet, who was in favour of the severance of Church from State.

In Milton's *Areopagitica: a Speech for the Liberty of Unlicensed Printing* (1644), the freedom of the press is eloquently sustained by arguments which are valid for freedom of thought in general. It is shown that the censorship will conduce 'to the discouragement of all learning and the stop of truth, not only by dis-exercising and blunting our abilities in what we know already, but by hindering and cropping the discovery that might be yet further made, both in religious and civil wisdom'. For knowledge is advanced through the utterance of new opinions, and truth is discovered by free discussion. If the waters of truth 'flow not in a perpetual progression they sicken into a muddy pool of conformity and tradition.' Books which are author-ized by the licensers are apt to be, as Bacon said, 'But the language of the times', and do not contribute to progress. The examples of the countries where the censorship is severe do not suggest that it is useful for morals: 'look into Italy and Spain, whether those places be one scruple the better, the honester, the wiser, the chaster, since all the inquisitional rigour that hath been executed upon books'. Spain indeed could reply, 'We are, what is more important, more orthodox.' It is interesting to notice that Milton places freedom of thought above civil liberty: 'Give me the liberty to know, to utter, and to argue freely according to con-science, above all other liberties.'

With the restoration of the Monarchy and the

Anglican Church, religious liberty was extinguished[1] by a series of laws against Dissenters. To the Revolution we owe the Act of Toleration (1689) from which the religious freedom which England enjoys at present is derived. It granted freedom of worship to Presbyterians, Congregationalists, Baptists, and Quakers, but only to these; Catholics and Unitarians were expressly excepted and the repressive legislation of Charles II remained in force against them. It was a characteristically English measure, logically inconsistent and absurd, a mixture of tolerance and intolerance, but suitable to the circumstances and the state of public opinion at the time.

In the same year John Locke's famous (first) *Letter concerning Toleration* appeared in Latin. Three subsequent letters developed and illustrated his thesis. The main argument is based on the principle that the business of civil government is quite distinct from that of religion, that the State is a society constituted only for preserving and promoting the civil interests of its members—civil interests meaning life, liberty, health, and the possession of property. The care of souls is not committed to magistrates more than to other men. For the magistrate can only use outward force; but

[1]There is reason to think that the aggressive anglicanism of the Restoration parliament was aggravated by the Catholic sympathies of Charles, and was in part a political defence against the real danger of Catholic absolutism; that the persecution of religious opinion, therefore, was partly parliament's declaration of independence. For a recent summary of the complicated debate which issued in the triumph of toleration, see *From Puritanism to the Age of Reason* by G. R. Cragg (C.U.P., 1950), chapter ix.—H.J.B.

true religion means the inward persuasion of the mind, and the mind is so made that force cannot compel it to believe. So too it is absurd for a State to make laws to enforce a religion, for laws are useless without penalties, and penalties are impertinent because they cannot convince.

Moreover, even if penalties could change men's beliefs, this would not conduce to the salvation of souls. Would more men be saved if all blindly resigned themselves to the will of their rulers and accepted the religion of their country? For as the princes of the world are divided in religion, one country alone would be in the right, and all the rest of the world would have to follow *their* princes to destruction; 'and that which heightens the absurdity, and very ill suits the notion of a deity, men would owe their eternal happiness or their eternal misery to the places of their nativity'. This is a principle on which Locke repeatedly insists. If a State is justified in imposing a creed, it follows that in all the lands except the one or few in which the true faith prevails, it is the duty of the subjects to embrace a false religion. If Protestantism is promoted in England, Popery by the same rule will be promoted in France. 'What is true and good in England will be true and good at Rome too, in China, or Geneva.' Toleration is the principle which gives to the true faith the best chance of prevailing.

Locke would concede full liberty to idolaters, by whom he means the Indians of North America, and he makes some scathing remarks on the ecclesiastical zeal which forced these 'innocent pagans' to forsake their ancient religion. But his toleration, though it extends beyond the Christian pale, is not complete. He excepts in the first place Roman Catholics, not on account of their theological dogmas but because they 'teach that faith is not to be kept with heretics', that 'kings excommunicated forfeit their crowns and kingdoms', and because they deliver themselves up to the protection and service of a foreign prince—the Pope. In other words, they are politically dangerous. His other exception is atheists. 'Those are not all to be tolerated who deny the being of God. Promises, covenants and oaths, which are the bonds of human society, can have no hold upon an atheist. The taking away of God, though but even in thought, dissolves all. Besides also, those that by their atheism undermine and destroy all religion, can have no pretence of religion to challenge the privilege of a Toleration.'

Thus Locke is not free from the prejudices of his time. These exceptions contradict his own principle that 'it is absurd that things should be enjoined by laws which are not in men's power to perform. And to believe this or that to be true does not depend upon our will.' This applies to Roman Catholics as to Protestants, to atheists as to deists. Locke, however, perhaps thought that the speculative opinion of atheism, which was uncommon in his day, does depend on the will. He would have excluded from his State his great contemporary Spinoza.

But in spite of its limitations Locke's *Toleration* is a work of the highest value, and its argument takes us further than its author went. It asserts unrestrictedly the secular principle, and its logical issue is Disestablishment. A Church is merely 'a free and voluntary society'. I may notice the remark that if infidels were to be converted by force, it was easier for God to do it 'with armies of heavenly legions than for any son of the Church, how potent soever, with all his dragoons'. This is a polite way of stating a maxim analogous to that of the Emperor Tiberius (above, p. 28). If false beliefs are an offence to God, it is, really, his affair.

The toleration of Nonconformists was far from pleasing extreme Anglicans, and the influence of this party at the beginning of the eighteenth century menaced the liberty of Dissenters. The situation provoked Defoe, who was a zealous Nonconformist, to write his pamphlet, *The Shortest Way with the Dissenters* (1702), an ironical attack upon the principle of toleration. It pretends to show that the Dissenters are at heart incorrigible rebels, that a gentle policy is useless, and suggests that all preachers at conventicles should be hanged and all persons found attending such meetings should be banished. This exceedingly amusing but terribly earnest caricature of the sentiments of the High Anglican party at first deceived and alarmed the Dissenters themselves. But the High Churchmen were furious. Defoe was fined, exposed in the pillory three times, and sent to Newgate prison.

But the Tory reaction was only temporary. During the eighteenth century, a relatively tolerant spirit prevailed among the Christian sects and new sects were founded. The official Church became less fanatical; many of its leading divines were influenced by rationalistic thought. If it had not been for the opposition of King George III, the Catholics might have been freed from their disabilities before the end of the century. This measure, eloquently advocated by Burke, and desired by Pitt, was not carried till 1829 and then under the threat of a revolution in Ireland. In the meantime legal toleration had been extended to the Unitarians in 1813, but they were not relieved from all disabilities till the forties. Jews were not admitted to the full rights of citizenship till 1858.

The achievement of religious liberty in England in the nineteenth century has been mainly the work of Liberals. The Liberal party has been moving towards the ultimate goal of complete secularization and the separation of the Church from the State— the logical results of Locke's theory of civil government. The Disestablishment of the Church in Ireland in 1869 partly realized this ideal, and now more than forty years later [1913] the Liberal party is seeking to apply the principle to Wales. It is highly characteristic of English politics and English psychology that the change should be carried out in this piecemeal fashion. In the other countries of the British Empire the system of Separation prevails; there is no connexion between the State and any sect; no Church is anything more than a voluntary society. But secularization has advanced under the State Church system. It is enough to mention the Education Act of 1870 and the abolition of religious tests at Universities (1871). Other gains for freedom will be noticed when I come to speak in another chapter of the progress of rationalism.

If we compare the religious situation in France in the seventeenth with that in the eighteenth century, it seems to be sharply contrasted with the development in England. In England there was a great advance towards religious liberty, in France there was a falling away. Until 1676 the French Protestants (Huguenots) were tolerated; for the next hundred years they were outlaws. But the toleration, which their charter (the Edict of Nantes, 1598) secured them, was of a limited kind. They were excluded, for instance, from the army; they were excluded from Paris and other cities and districts. And the liberty which they enjoyed was confined to them; it was not granted to any other sect. The charter was faithfully maintained by the two great cardinals (Richelieu and Mazarin) who governed France under Louis XIII and Louis XIV, but when the latter assumed the active power in 1661 he began a series of laws against the Protestants which culminated in the revoking of the charter (1676) and the beginning of a Protestant persecution.

The French clergy justified this policy by the notorious text 'Compel them to come in', and appealed to St. Augustine. Their arguments evoked a defence of toleration by Bayle, a French Protestant who had taken refuge in Holland. It was entitled a *Philosophical Commentary on the text 'Compel them to come in'* (1686) and in importance stands beside Locke's work which was being composed at the same time. Many of the arguments urged by the two writers are identical. They agreed, and for the same reasons, in excluding Roman Catholics. The most characteristic thing in

Bayle's treatise is his sceptical argument that, even if it were a right principle to suppress error by force, no truth is certain enough to justify us in applying the theory. We shall see (next chapter) this eminent scholar's contribution to rationalism.

Though there was an immense exodus of Protestants from France, Louis did not succeed in his design of extirpating heresy from his lands. In the eighteenth century under Louis xv, the presence of Protestants was tolerated though they were outlaws; their marriages were not recognized as legal, and they were liable at any moment to persecution. About the middle of the century, a literary agitation began, conducted mainly by rationalists, but finally supported by enlightened Catholics, to relieve the affliction of the oppressed sect. It resulted at last in an Edict of Toleration (1787), which made the position of the Protestants endurable, though it excluded them from certain careers.

The most energetic and forceful leader in the campaign against intolerance was Voltaire (see next chapter) and his exposure of some glaring cases of unjust persecution did more than general arguments to achieve the object. The most infamous case was that of Jean Calas, a Protestant merchant of Toulouse, whose son committed suicide. A report was set abroad that the young man had decided to join the Catholic Church, and that his father, mother and brother, filled with Protestant bigotry, killed him, with the help of a friend. They were all put in irons, tried, and condemned, though there were no arguments for their guilt, except the conjecture of bigotry. Jean Calas was broken on the wheel, his son and daughter cast into convents, his wife left to starve. Through the activity of Voltaire, then living near Geneva, the widow was induced to go to Paris, where she was kindly received, and assisted by eminent lawyers; a judicial inquiry was made; the Toulouse sentence was reversed and the King granted pensions to those who had suffered. This scandal could only have happened in the provinces, according to Voltaire: 'at Paris,' he says, 'fanaticism, powerful though it may be, is always controlled by reason'.

The case of Sirven, though it did not end tragically, was similar, and the government of Toulouse was again responsible. He was accused of having drowned his daughter in a well to hinder her from becoming a Catholic, and was, with his wife, sentenced to death. Fortunately he and his family had escaped to Switzerland, where they persuaded Voltaire of their innocence. To get the sentence reversed was the work of nine years and this time it was reversed at Toulouse. When Voltaire visited Paris in 1778, he was acclaimed by crowds as the 'defender of Calas and the Sirvens'. His disinterested practical activity against persecution was of far more value than the treatise on *Toleration* which he wrote in connexion with the Calas episode. It is a poor work compared with those of Locke and Bayle. The tolerance which he advocates is of a limited kind; he would confine public offices and dignities to those who belong to the State religion.

But if Voltaire's system of toleration is limited, it is wide compared with the religious establishment advocated by his contemporary, Rousseau. Though of Swiss birth, Rousseau belongs to the literature and history of France; but it was not for nothing that he was brought up in the traditions of Calvinistic Geneva. His ideal State would, in its way, have been little better than any theocracy. He proposed to establish a 'civil religion' which was to be a sort of undogmatic Christianity. But certain dogmas, which he considered essential, were to be imposed on all citizens on pain of banishment. Such were the existence of a deity, the future bliss of the good and punishment of the bad, the duty of tolerance towards all those who accepted the fundamental articles of faith. It may be said that a State founded on this basis would be fairly inclusive —that all Christian sects and many deists could find a place in it. But by imposing indispensable beliefs, it denies the principle of toleration. The importance of Rousseau's idea lies in the fact that it inspired one of the experiments in religious policy which were made during the French Revolution.

The Revolution established religious liberty in France. Most of the leaders were unorthodox. Their rationalism was naturally of the eighteenth-century type, and in the preamble to the Declaration of Rights (1789) deism was asserted by the words 'in the presence and under the auspices of the Supreme Being' (against which only one voice protested). The Declaration laid down that no one was to be vexed on account of his religious opinions provided he did not thereby trouble public order. Catholicism was retained as the 'domi-nant' religion; Protestants (but not Jews) were admitted

to public office. Mirabeau, the greatest statesman of
the day, protested strongly against the use of words
like 'tolerance' and 'dominant'. He said: 'The most
unlimited liberty of religion is in my eyes a right so
sacred that to express it by the word toleration seems
to me itself a sort of tyranny, since the authority which
tolerates might also not tolerate.' The same protest
was made in Thomas Paine's *Rights of Man* which
appeared two years later: 'Toleration is not the *opposite*
of Intolerance, but is the *counterfeit* of it. Both are
despotisms. The one assumes itself the right of with-
holding liberty of conscience, and the other of granting
it.' Paine was an ardent deist, and he added: 'Were a
bill brought into any parliament, entitled "An Act to
tolerate or grant liberty to the Almighty to receive the
worship of a Jew or a Turk," or "to prohibit the
Almighty from receiving it," all men would startle
and call it blasphemy. There would be an uproar. The
presumption of toleration in religious matters would
then present itself unmasked.'

The Revolution began well, but the spirit of Mirabeau was not in the ascendant throughout its course.
The vicissitudes in religious policy from 1789 to 1801
have a particular interest, because they show that the
principle of liberty of conscience was far from possess-
ing the minds of the men who were proud of abolishing
the intolerance of the government which they had
overthrown. The State Church was reorganized by the
Civil Constitution of the Clergy (1790), by which
French citizens were forbidden to acknowledge the
authority of the Pope and the appointment of bishops

was transferred to the Electors of the Departments, so that the commanding influence passed from the Crown to the nation. Doctrine and worship were not touched. Under the democratic Republic which succeeded the fall of the monarchy (1792–5) this Constitution was maintained, but a movement to dechristianize France was inaugurated, and the Commune of Paris ordered the churches of all religions to be closed. The worship of Reason, with rites modelled on the Catholic, was organized in Paris and the provinces. The government, violently anti-Catholic, did not care to use force against the prevalent faith; direct persecution would have weakened the national defence and scandalized Europe. They naïvely hoped that the superstition would disappear by degrees. Robespierre declared against the policy of unchristianizing France, and when he had the power (April 1795), he established as a State religion the worship of the Supreme Being. 'The French people recognizes the existence of the Supreme Being and the immortality of the Soul'; the liberty of other cults was maintained. Thus, for a few months, Rousseau's idea was more or less realized. It meant intolerance. Atheism was regarded as a vice, and 'all were atheists, who did not think like Robespierre'.

The democratic was succeeded by the middle-class Republic (1795–9), and the policy of its government was to hinder the preponderance of any one religious group; to hold the balance among all the creeds, but with a certain partiality against the strongest, the Catholic, which threatened, as was thought, to destroy the others or even the Republic. The plan was to favour the growth of new rationalistic cults, and to undermine revealed religion by a secular system of education. Accordingly the Church was separated from the State by the Constitution of 1795, which affirmed the liberty of all worship and withdrew from the Catholic clergy the salaries which the State had hitherto paid. The elementary schools were laicized. The Declaration of Rights, the articles of the Constitution, and republican morality were taught instead of religion. An enthusiast declared that 'the religion of Socrates, Marcus Aurelius and Cicero would soon be the religion of the world'.

A new rationalistic religion was introduced under the name of Theophilanthropy. It was the 'natural religion' of the philosophers and poets of the century, of Voltaire and the English deists—not the purified Christianity of Rousseau, but anterior and superior to Christianity. Its doctrines, briefly formulated were: God, immortality, fraternity, humanity; no attacks on other religions, but respect and honour towards all; gatherings in a family, or in a temple, to encourage one another to practise morality. Protected by the government sometimes secretly, sometimes openly, it had a certain success among the cultivated classes.

The idea of the lay State was popularized under this rule, and by the end of the century there was virtually religious peace in France. Under the Consulate (from 1799) the same system continued, but Napoleon ceased to protect Theophilanthropy. In 1801, though there seems to have been little discontent with the existing arrangement, Napoleon decided to upset it and bring the Pope upon the scene. The Catholic religion, as that of the majority, was again taken under the special protection of the State, the salaries of the clergy again paid by the nation, and the papal authority over the Church again recognized within well-defined limits; while full toleration of other religions was maintained. This was the effect of the concordat between the French Republic and the Pope. It is the judgement of a high authority that the nation, if it had been consulted, would have pronounced against the change. It may be doubted whether this is true. But Napoleon's policy seems to have been prompted by the calculation that, using the Pope as an instrument, he could control the consciences of men, and more easily carry out his plans of empire.

Apart from its ecclesiastical policies and its experiments in new creeds based on the principles of rationalistic thinkers, the French Revolution itself has an interest, in connexion with our subject, as an example of the coercion of reason by an intolerant faith.

The leaders believed that, by applying certain principles, they could regenerate France and show the world how the lasting happiness of mankind can be secured. They acted in the name of reason, but their principles were articles of faith, which were accepted just as blindly and irrationally as the dogmas of any supernatural creed. One of these dogmas was the false doctrine of Rousseau that man is a being who is naturally good and loves justice and order. Another was the illusion that all men are equal by nature. The puerile conviction prevailed that legislation could completely blot out the past and radically transform the character of a society. 'Liberty, equality, and fraternity'. was as much a creed as the Creed of the Apostles; it hypnotized men's minds like a revelation from on high; and reason had as little part in its propagation as in the spread of Christianity or of Protestantism. It meant anything but equality, fraternity, or liberty, especially liberty, when it was translated into action by the fanatical apostles of 'Reason', who were blind to the facts of human nature and defied the facts of economics. Terror, the usual instrument in propagating religions, was never more mercilessly applied. Any one who questioned the doctrines was a heretic and deserved a heretic's fate. And, as in most religious movements, the milder and less unreasonable spirits succumbed to the fanatics. Never was the name of reason more grievously abused than by those who believed they were inaugurating her reign.

Religious liberty, however, among other good things, did emerge from the Revolution, at first in the form of Separation, and then under the concordat. The concordat lasted for more than a century, under monarchies and republics, till it was abolished in December 1905, when the system of Separation was introduced again.

In the German States the history of religious liberty differs in many ways, but it resembles the development in France in so far as toleration in a limited form was at first brought about by war. The Thirty Years' War, which divided Germany in the first half of the seventeenth century, and in which, as in the English Civil

War, religion and politics were mixed, was terminated by the Peace of Westphalia (1648). By this act, three religions, the Catholic, the Lutheran, and the Reformed[1] were legally recognized by the Holy Roman Empire, and placed on an equality; all other religions were excluded. But it was left to each of the German States, of which the Empire consisted, to tolerate or not any religion it pleased. That is, every prince could impose on his subjects whichever of the three religions he chose, and refuse to tolerate the others in his territory. But he might also admit one or both of the others, and he might allow the followers of other creeds to reside in his dominion, and practise their religions within the precincts of their own houses. Thus toleration varied, from State to State, according to the policy of each particular prince.

As elsewhere, so in Germany, considerations of political expediency promoted the growth of toleration, especially in Prussia; and as elsewhere, theoretical advocates exercised great influence on public opinion. But the case for toleration was based by its German defenders chiefly on legal, not, as in England and France, on moral and intellectual grounds. They regarded it as a question of law, and discussed it from the point of view of the legal relations between State and Church. It had been considered long ago from this standpoint by an original Italian thinker, Marsilius of Padua (thirteenth century), who had maintained that the Church had no power to employ physical

[1]The Reformed Church consists of the followers of Calvin and Zwingli.

coercion and that if the lay authority punished heretics, the punishment was inflicted for the violation not of divine ordinances but of the law of the State, which excluded heretics from its territory.

Christian Thomasius may be taken as a leading exponent of the theory that religious liberty logically follows from a right conception of law. He laid down in a series of pamphlets (1693–7) that the prince, who alone has the power of coercion, has no right to interfere in spiritual matters, while the clergy step beyond their province if they interfere in secular matters or defend their faith by any other means than teaching. But the secular power has no legal right to coerce heretics unless heresy is a crime. And heresy is not a crime, but an error; for it is not a matter of will. Thomasius, moreover, urges the view that the public welfare has nothing to gain from unity of faith, that it makes no difference what faith a man professes so long as he is loyal to the State. His toleration indeed is not complete. He was much influenced by the writings of his contemporary Locke, and he excepts from the benefit of toleration the same classes which Locke excepted.

Besides the influence of the jurists, we may note that the Pietistic movement—a reaction of religious enthusiasm against the formal theology of the Lutheran divines—was animated by a spirit favourable to toleration; and that the cause was promoted by the leading men of letters, especially by Lessing, in the second half of the eighteenth century.

But perhaps the most important fact of all in hastening the realization of religious liberty in Germany was the accession of a rationalist to the throne of Prussia, in the person of Frederick the Great. A few months after his accession (1740) he wrote in the margin of a State paper, in which a question of religious policy occurred, that every one should be allowed to get to heaven in his own way. His view that morality was independent of religion and therefore compatible with all religions, and that thus a man could be a good citizen—the only thing which the State was entitled to demand—whatever faith he might profess, led to the logical consequence of complete religious liberty. Catholics were placed on an equality with Protestants, and the Treaty of Westphalia was violated by the extension of full toleration to all the forbidden sects. Frederick even conceived the idea of introducing Mohammadan settlers into some parts of his realm. Contrast England under George III, France under Louis XV, Italy under the shadow of the Popes. It is an important fact in history, which has hardly been duly emphasized, that full *religious* liberty was for the first time, in any country in modern Europe, realized under a freethinking ruler, the friend of the great 'blasphemer' Voltaire.

The policy and principles of Frederick were formulated in the Prussian Territorial Code of 1794, by which unrestricted liberty of conscience was guaranteed, and the three chief religions, the Lutheran, the Reformed, and the Catholic, were placed on the same footing and enjoyed the same privileges. The system is 'jurisdictional'; only, three Churches here occupy

the position which the Anglican Church alone occupies
in England. The rest of Germany did not begin to
move in the direction pointed out by Prussia until, by
one of the last acts of the Holy Roman Empire (1803),
the Westphalian settlement had been modified. Before
the foundation of the new Empire (1870), freedom was
established throughout Germany.

In Austria, the Emperor Joseph II issued an Edict
of Toleration in 1781, which may be considered a
broad measure for a Catholic State at that time.
Joseph was a sincere Catholic, but he was not imper-
vious to the enlightened ideas of his age; he was an
admirer of Frederick, and his edict was prompted by a
genuinely tolerant spirit, such as had not inspired the
English Act of 1689. It extended only to the Lutheran
and Reformed sects and the communities of the Greek
Church which had entered into union with Rome, and
it was of a limited kind. Religious liberty was not
established till 1867.

The measure of Joseph applied to the Austrian
States in Italy, and helped to prepare that country for
the idea of religious freedom. It is notable that in Italy
in the eighteenth century toleration found its advocate,
not in a rationalist or a philosopher, but in a Catholic
ecclesiastic, Tamburini, who (under the name of his
friend Trautmansdorf) published a work *On Ecclesiastical and Civil Toleration* (1783). A sharp line is drawn
between the provinces of the Church and the State,
persecution and the Inquisition are condemned, coercion of conscience is declared inconsistent with the
Christian spirit, and the principle is laid down that the

sovran should only exercise coercion where the interests of public safety are concerned. Like Locke, the author thinks that atheism is a legitimate case for such coercion.

The new States which Napoleon set up in Italy exhibited toleration in various degrees, but real liberty was first introduced in Piedmont by Cavour (1848), a measure which prepared the way for the full liberty which was one of the first-fruits of the foundation of the Italian kingdom in 1870. The union of Italy, with all that it meant, is the most signal and dramatic act in the triumph of the ideas of the modern State over the traditional principles of the Christian Church. Rome, which preserved those principles most faithfully, has offered a steadfast, we may say a heroic, resistance to the liberal ideas which swept Europe in the nineteenth century. The guides of her policy grasped thoroughly the danger which liberal thought meant for an institution which, founded in a remote past, claimed to be unchangeable and never out of date. Gregory XVI issued a solemn protest maintaining authority against freedom, the mediaeval against the modern ideal, in an Encyclical Letter (1832), which was intended as a rebuke to some young French Catholics (Lamennais and his friends) who had conceived the promising idea of transforming the Church by the Liberal spirit of the day. The Pope denounces 'the absurd and erroneous maxim, or rather insanity, that liberty of conscience should be procured and guaranteed to every one. The path to this pernicious error is prepared by that full and unlimited liberty of thought which is spread abroad to the misfortune of Church and State and which certain persons, with excessive impudence, venture to represent as an advantage for religion. Hence comes the corruption of youth, contempt for religion and for the most venerable laws, and a general mental change in the world—in short the most deadly scourge of society; since the experience of history has shown that the States which have shone by their wealth and power and glory have perished just by this evil—immoderate freedom of opinion, licence of conversation, and love of novelties. With this is connected the liberty of publishing any writing of any kind. This is a deadly and execrable liberty for which we cannot feel sufficient horror, though some men dare to acclaim it noisily and enthusiastically.' A generation later Pius IX was to astonish the world by a similar manifesto—his Syllabus of Modern Errors (1864). Yet, notwithstanding the fundamental antagonism between the principles of the Church and the drift of modern civilization, the Papacy survives, powerful and respected, in a world where the ideas which it condemned have become the commonplace conditions of life.

The progress of western nations from the system of unity which prevailed in the fifteenth, to the system of liberty which was the rule in the nineteenth century, was slow and painful, illogical and wavering, generally dictated by political necessities, seldom inspired by deliberate conviction. We have seen how religious liberty has been realized, so far as the law is concerned, under two distinct systems, 'Jurisdiction' and

'Separation'. But legal toleration may coexist with much practical intolerance, and liberty before the law is compatible with serious disabilities of which the law cannot take account. For instance, the expression of unorthodox opinions may exclude a man from obtaining a secular post or hinder his advancement. The question has been asked, which of the two systems is more favourable to the creation of a tolerant social atmosphere. Ruffini (of whose excellent work on *Religious Liberty* I have made much use in this chapter) decides in favour of Jurisdiction. He points out that while Socinus, a true friend of liberty of thought, contemplated this system, the Anabaptists, whose spirit was intolerant, sought Separation. More important is the observation that in Germany, England, and Italy, where the most powerful Church or Churches are under the control of the State, there is more freedom, more tolerance of opinion, than in many of the American States where Separation prevails. A hundred years ago the Americans showed appalling ingratitude to Thomas Paine, who had done them eminent service in the War of Independence, simply because he published a very unorthodox book. It is notorious that free thought is still a serious hindrance and handicap to an American, even in most of the universities. This proves that Separation is not an infallible receipt for producing tolerance. But I see no reason to suppose that public opinion in America would be different, if either the Federal Republic or the particular States had adopted Jurisdiction. Given legal liberty under either system, I should say that the tolerance of public opinion depends on social conditions and especially on the degree of culture among the educated classes.

From this sketch it will be seen that toleration was the outcome of new political circumstances and necessities, brought about by the disunion of the Church through the Reformation. But it meant that in those States which granted toleration the opinion of a sufficiently influential group of the governing class was ripe for the change, and this new mental attitude was in a great measure due to the scepticism and rationalism which were diffused by the Renaissance movement, and which subtly and unconsciously had affected the minds of many who were sincerely devoted to rigidly orthodox beliefs; so effective is the force of suggestion. In the next two chapters the advance of reason at the expense of faith will be traced through the seventeenth, eighteenth, and nineteenth centuries.

Chapter VI

THE GROWTH OF RATIONALISM: SEVENTEENTH AND EIGHTEENTH CENTURIES

DURING the last 300 years reason has been slowly but steadily destroying Christian mythology and exposing the pretensions of supernatural revelation. The progress of rationalism falls naturally into two periods. (1) In the seventeenth and eighteenth centuries those thinkers who rejected Christian theology and the book on which it relies were mainly influenced by the inconsistencies, contradictions, and absurdities which they discovered in the evidence, and by the moral difficulties of the creed. Some scientific facts were known which seemed to reflect on the accuracy of Revelation, but arguments based on science were subsidiary. (2) In the nineteenth century the discoveries of science in many fields bore with full force upon fabrics which had been constructed in a naïve and ignorant age; and historical criticism undermined methodically the authority of the sacred documents which had hitherto been exposed chiefly to the acute but unmethodical criticisms of common sense.

A disinterested love of facts, without any regard to the bearing which those facts may have on one's hopes or fears or destiny, is a rare quality in all ages, and it had been very rare indeed since the ancient days of Greece and Rome. It means the scientific spirit. Now

in the seventeenth century we may say (without dis-
respect to a few precursors) that the modern study of
natural science began, and in the same period we have
a series of famous thinkers who were guided by a disinterested love of truth. Of the most acute minds some
reached the conclusion that the Christian scheme of
the world is irrational, and according to their tempera-
ment some rejected it, whilst others, like the great
Frenchman Pascal, fell back upon an unreasoning act
of faith. Bacon, who professed orthodoxy, was perhaps
at heart a deist, but in any case the whole spirit of his
writings was to exclude authority from the domain of
scientific investigation which he did so much to
stimulate. Descartes, illustrious not only as the founder
of modern metaphysics but also by his original contributions to science, might seek to conciliate the
ecclesiastical authorities—his temper was timid—but
his philosophical method was a powerful incentive to
rationalistic thought. The general tendency of superior
intellects was to exalt reason at the expense of authority;
and in England this principle was established so firmly
by Locke, that throughout the theological warfare of
the eighteenth century both parties relied on reason,
and no theologian of repute assumed faith to be a
higher faculty.

A striking illustration of the gradual encroachments
of reason is the change which was silently wrought in
public opinion on the subject of witchcraft. The
famous efforts of James I to carry out the Biblical
command, 'Thou shalt not suffer a witch to live', were
outdone by the zeal of the Puritans under the Com-

monwealth to suppress the wicked old women who had commerce with Satan. After the Restoration, the belief in witchcraft declined among educated people—though some able writers maintained it—and there were few executions. The last trial of a witch was in 1712, when some clergymen in Hertfordshire prosecuted Jane Wenham. The jury found her guilty, but the judge, who had summed up in her favour, was able to procure the remission of her sentence; and the laws against witchcraft were repealed in 1735. John Wesley said with perfect truth that to disbelieve in witchcraft is to disbelieve in the Bible. In France and in Holland the decline of belief and interest in this particular form of Satan's activity was simultaneous. In Scotland, where theology was very powerful, a woman was burnt in 1722. It can be no mere coincidence that the general decline of this superstition belongs to the age which saw the rise of modern science and modern philosophy.

Hobbes, who was perhaps the most brilliant English thinker of the seventeenth century, was a freethinker and materialist. He had come under the influence of his friend the French philosopher Gassendi, who had revived materialism in its Epicurean shape. Yet he was a champion not of freedom of conscience but of coercion in its most uncompromising form. In the political theory which he expounded in *Leviathan*, the sovran has autocratic power in the domain of doctrine, as in everything else, and it is the duty of subjects to conform to the religion which the sovran imposes. Religious persecution is thus defended, but no independent power is left to the Church. But the principles on which Hobbes built up his theory were rationalistic. He separated morality from religion and identified 'the true moral philosophy' with the 'true doctrine of the laws of nature'. What he really thought of religion could be inferred from his remark that the fanciful fear of things invisible (due to ignorance) is the natural seed of that feeling which, in himself, a man calls religion, but, in those who fear or worship the invisible power differently, superstition. In the reign of Charles ii Hobbes was silenced and his books were burned.

Spinoza, the Jewish philosopher of Holland, owed a great deal to Descartes and (in political speculation) to Hobbes, but his philosophy meant a far wider and more open breach with orthodox opinion than either of his masters had ventured on. He conceived ultimate reality, which he called God, as an absolutely perfect, *impersonal* Being, a substance whose nature is constituted by two 'attributes'—thought and spatial extension. When Spinoza speaks of love of God, in which he considered happiness to consist, he means knowledge and contemplation of the order of nature, including human nature, which is subject to fixed, invariable laws. He rejects free-will and the 'superstition', as he calls it, of final causes in nature. If we want to label his philosophy, we may say that it is a form of pantheism. It has often been described as atheism. If atheism means, as I suppose in ordinary use it is generally taken to mean, rejection of a personal God, Spinoza was an atheist. It should be observed that in the seventeenth and eighteenth centuries atheist was used in the wildest way as a term of abuse for freethinkers, and when we read of atheists (except in careful writers) we may generally assume that the persons so stigmatized were really deists, that is, they believed in a personal God but not in Revelation.[1]

Spinoza's daring philosophy was not in harmony with the general trend of speculation at the time, and did not exert any profound influence on thought till a much later period. The thinker whose writings appealed most to the men of his age and were most opportune and effective was John Locke, who professed more or less orthodox Anglicanism. His great contribution to philosophy is equivalent to a very powerful defence of reason against the usurpations of authority. The object of his *Essay on the Human Understanding* (1690) is to show that all knowledge is derived from experience. He subordinated faith completely to reason. While he accepted the Christian revelation, he held that revelation if it contradicted the higher tribunal of reason must be rejected, and that revelation cannot give us knowledge as certain as the knowledge which reason gives. 'He that takes away reason to make room for revelation puts out the light of both; and does much what the same as if he would persuade a man to put out his eyes, the better to receive the remote light of an invisible star by a telescope.' He wrote a book to show that the Christian revelation is not contrary to reason, and its title, *The Reasonableness of Christianity*,

[1]For the sake of simplicity I use deist in this sense throughout, though theist is now the usual term.

H

sounds the note of all religious controversy in England during the next hundred years. Both the orthodox and their opponents warmly agreed that reasonableness was the only test of the claims of revealed religion.

It was under the direct influence of Locke that Toland, an Irishman who had been converted from Roman Catholicism, composed a sensational book, *Christianity Not Mysterious* (1696). He assumes that Christianity is true and argues that there can be no mysteries in it, because mysteries, that is, unintelligible dogmas, cannot be accepted by reason. And if a reasonable Deity gave a revelation, its purpose must be to enlighten, not to puzzle. The assumption of the truth of Christianity was a mere pretence, as an intelligent reader could not fail to see. The work was important because it drew the logical inference from Locke's philosophy, and it had a wide circulation. Lady Mary Wortley Montagu met a Turkish *effendi* at Belgrade who asked her for news of Mr. Toland.

It is characteristic of this stage of the struggle between reason and authority that (excepting the leading French thinkers in the eighteenth century) the rationalists, who attacked theology, generally feigned to acknowledge the truth of the ideas which they were assailing. They pretended that their speculations did not affect religion; they could separate the domains of reason and of faith; they could show that Revelation was superfluous without questioning it; they could do homage to orthodoxy and lay down views with which orthodoxy was irreconcilable. The errors which they exposed in the sphere of reason were ironically allowed to be truths in the sphere of theology. The mediaeval principle of double truth and other shifts were resorted to, in self-protection against the tyranny of orthodoxy—though they did not always avail; and in reading much of the rationalistic literature of this period we have to read between the lines. Bayle is an interesting instance.

If Locke's philosophy, by setting authority in its place and deriving all knowledge from experience, was a powerful aid to rationalism, his contemporary Bayle worked in the same direction by the investigation of history. Driven from France (see above, p. 84), he lived at Amsterdam, where he published his *Philosophical Dictionary*. He was really a freethinker, but he never dropped the disguise of orthodoxy, and this lends a particular piquancy to his work. He takes a delight in marshalling all the objections which heretics had made to essential Christian dogmas. He exposed without mercy the crimes and brutalities of David, and showed that this favourite of the Almighty was a person with whom one would refuse to shake hands. There was a great outcry at this unedifying candour. Bayle, in replying, adopted the attitude of Montaigne and Pascal, and opposed faith to reason.

The theological virtue of faith, he said, consists in believing revealed truths simply and solely on God's authority. If you believe in the immortality of the soul for philosophical reasons, you are orthodox, but you have no part in faith. The merit of faith becomes greater, in proportion as the revealed truth surpasses all the powers of our mind; the more incomprehensible the truth and the more repugnant to reason, the greater is the sacrifice we make in accepting it, the deeper our submission to God. Therefore a merciless inventory of the objections which reason has to urge against fundamental doctrines serves to exalt the merits of faith.

The *Dictionary* was also criticized for the justice done to the moral excellences of persons who denied the existence of God. Bayle replies that if he had been able to find any atheistical thinkers, who lived bad lives, he would have been delighted to dwell on their vices, but he knew of none such. As for the criminals you meet in history, whose abominable actions make you tremble, their impieties and blasphemies prove they believed in a Divinity. This is a natural consequence of the theological doctrine that the devil, who is incapable of atheism, is the instigator of all the sins of men. For man's wickedness must clearly resemble that of the devil and must therefore be joined to a belief in God's existence, since the devil is not an atheist. And is it not a proof of the infinite wisdom of God that the worst criminals are not atheists, and that most of the atheists whose names are recorded have been honest men? By this arrangement providence sets bounds to the corruption of man; for if atheism and moral wickedness were united in the same persons, the societies of earth would be exposed to a fatal inundation of sin.

There was much more in the same vein; and the upshot was, under the thin veil of serving faith, to show that the Christian dogmas were essentially unreasonable.

Bayle's work, marked by scholarship and extraordinary learning, had a great influence in England
as well as in France. It supplied weapons to assailants
of Christianity in both countries. At first the assault
was carried on with most vigour and ability by the
English deists, who, though their writings are little
read now, did memorable work by their polemic
against the authority of revealed religion.

The controversy between the deists and their orthodox opponents turned on the question whether the
Deity of natural religion—the God whose existence,
as was thought, could be proved by reason—can be
identified with the author of the Christian revelation.
To the deists this seemed impossible. The nature of
the alleged revelation seemed inconsistent with the
character of the God to whom reason pointed. The
defenders of revelation, at least all the most competent, agreed with the deists in making reason supreme,
and through this reliance on reason some of them fell
into heresies. Clarke, for instance, one of the ablest,
was very unsound on the dogma of the Trinity. It
is also to be noticed that with both sections the interest
of morality was the principal motive. The orthodox
held that the revealed doctrine of future rewards and
punishments is necessary for morality; the deists,
that morality depends on reason alone, and that
revelation contains a great deal that is repugnant to
moral ideals. Throughout the eighteenth century
morality was the guiding consideration with Anglican
Churchmen, and religious emotion, finding no satisfaction within the Church was driven, as it were,

outside, and sought an outlet in the Methodism of Wesley and Whitefield.

Spinoza had laid down the principle that Scripture must be interpreted like any other book (1670),[1] and with the deists this principle was fundamental. In order to avoid persecution they generally veiled their conclusions under sufficiently thin disguises. Hitherto the Press Licensing Act (1662) had very effectually prevented the publication of heterodox works, and it is from orthodox works denouncing infidel opinions that we know how rationalism was spreading. But in 1695, the press law was allowed to drop, and immediately deistic literature began to appear. There was, however, the danger of prosecution under the blasphemy laws. There were three legal weapons for coercing those who attacked Christianity: (1) The ecclesiastical courts had and have the power of imprisoning for a maximum term of six months, for atheism, blasphemy, heresy and damnable opinions. (2) The common law as interpreted by Lord Chief Justice Hale in 1676, when a certain Taylor was charged with having said that religion was a cheat and blasphemed against Christ. The accused was condemned to a fine and the pillory by the judge, who ruled that the Court of King's Bench has jurisdiction in such a case, inasmuch as blasphemous words of the kind are an offence against the laws and the State, and to speak against Christianity is to speak in subversion of the law, since

[1] Spinoza's *Theological Political Treatise*, which deals with the interpretation of Scripture, was translated into English in 1689.

Christianity is 'parcel of the laws of England'. (3) The statute of 1698 enacts that if any person educated in the Christian religion 'shall by writing, printing, teaching, or advised speaking deny any one of the persons in the Holy Trinity to be God, or shall assert or maintain there are more gods than one, or shall deny the Christian religion to be true, or shall deny the Holy Scriptures of the Old and New Testament to be of divine authority,' and is convicted, he shall for the first offence be adjudged incapable to hold any public offices or employments, and on the second shall lose his civil rights and be imprisoned for three years. This statute expressly states as its motive the fact that 'many persons have of late years openly avowed and published many blasphemous and impious opinions contrary to the doctrine and principles of the Christian religion'.

As a matter of fact, most trials for blasphemy during the past 200 years fall under the second head. But the new statute of 1698 was very intimidating, and we can easily understand how it drove heterodox writers to ambiguous disguises. One of these disguises was allegorical interpretation of Scripture. They showed that literal interpretation led to absurdities or to inconsistencies with the wisdom and justice of God, and pretended to infer that allegorical interpretation must be substituted. But they meant the reader to reject their pretended solution and draw a conclusion damaging to Revelation.

Among the arguments used in favour of the truth of Revelation the fulfilment of prophecies and the miracles of the New Testament were conspicuous. Anthony Collins, a country gentleman who was a disciple of Locke, published in 1733 his *Discourse on the Grounds and Reasons of the Christian Religion*, in which he drastically exposed the weakness of the evidence for fulfilment of prophecy, depending as it does on forced and unnatural figurative interpretations. Twenty years before he had written a *Discourse of Freethinking* (in which Bayle's influence is evident) pleading for free discussion and the reference of all religious questions to reason. He complained of the general intolerance which prevailed; but the same facts which testify to intolerance testify also to the spread of unbelief.

Collins escaped with comparative impunity, but Thomas Woolston, a Fellow of Sidney Sussex College, Cambridge, who wrote six aggressive *Discourses on the Miracles of our Saviour* (1727–30) paid the penalty for his audacity. Deprived of his Fellowship, he was prosecuted for libel, and sentenced to a fine of £100 and a year's imprisonment. Unable to pay, he died in prison. He does not adopt the line of arguing that miracles are incredible or impossible. He examines the chief miracles related in the Gospels, and shows with great ability and shrewd common sense that they are absurd or unworthy of the performer. He pointed out, as Huxley was to point out in a controversy with Gladstone, that the miraculous driving of devils into a herd of swine was an unwarrantable injury to some-body's property. On the story of the divine blasting of the fig tree, he remarks: 'What if a yeoman of Kent should go to look for pippins in his orchard at Easter (the supposed time that Jesus sought for these figs) and because of a disappointment cut down his trees? What then would his neighbours make of him? Nothing less than a laughing-stock; and if the story got into our Publick News, he would be the jest and ridicule of mankind.'

Or take his comment on the miracle of the Pool of Bethesda, where an angel used to trouble the waters and the man who first entered the pool was cured of his infirmity. 'An odd and a merry way of conferring a Divine mercy. And one would think that the angels of God did this for their own diversion more than to do good to mankind. Just as some throw a bone among a kennel of hounds for the pleasure of seeing them quarrel for it, or as others cast a piece of money among a company of boys for the sport of seeing them scramble for it, so was the pastime of the angels here.' In dealing with the healing of the woman who suffered from a bloody flux, he asks: 'What if we had been told of the Pope's curing an haemorrhage like this before us, what would Protestants have said to it? Why, "that a foolish, credulous and superstitious woman had fancied herself cured of some slight indisposition, and the crafty Pope and his adherents, aspiring after popular applause, magnified the presumed cure into a miracle". The application of such a supposed story of a miracle wrought by the Pope is easy; and if Infidels, Jews and Mahometans, who have no better opinion of Jesus than we have of the Pope, should make it, there's no help for it.'

Woolston professed no doubts of the inspiration of Scripture. While he argued that it was out of the question to suppose the miracles literally true, he pretended to believe in the fantastic theory that they were intended allegorically as figures of Christ's mysterious operations in the soul of man. Origen, a not very orthodox Christian Father, had employed the allegorical method, and Woolston quotes him in his favour. His vigorous criticisms vary in value, but many of them hit the nail on the head, and the fashion of some modern critics to pass over Woolston's productions as unimportant because they are 'ribald' or 'coarse', is perfectly unjust. The pamphlets had an enormous sale, and Woolston's notoriety is illustrated by the anecdote of the 'jolly young woman' who met him walking abroad and accosted him with 'You old rogue, are you not hanged yet?' Mr. Woolston answered, 'Good woman, I know you not; pray what have I done to offend you?' 'You have writ against my Saviour,' she said; 'what would become of my poor sinful soul if it was not for my dear Saviour?'

About the same time, Matthew Tindal (a Fellow of All Souls) attacked Revelation from a more general point of view. In his *Christianity as old as the Creation* (1730) he undertook to show that the Bible as a revelation is superfluous, for it adds nothing to natural religion, which God revealed to man from the very first by the sole light of reason. He argues that those who defend Revealed religion by its agreement with Natural religion, and thus set up a double government of reason and authority, fall between the two. 'It's an odd jumble', he observes, 'to prove the truth of a book by the truth of the doctrines it contains, and at the same time conclude those doctrines to be true because contained in that book.' He goes on to criticize the Bible in detail. In order to maintain its infallibility, without doing violence to reason, you have, when you find irrational statements, to torture them and depart from the literal sense. Would you think that a Mohammadan was governed by his Koran, who on all occasions departed from the literal sense? 'Nay, would you not tell him that his inspired book fell infinitely short of Cicero's uninspired writings, where there is no such occasion to recede from the letter?'

As to chronological and physical errors, which seemed to endanger the infallibility of the Scriptures, a bishop had met the argument by saying, reasonably enough, that in the Bible God speaks according to the conceptions of those to whom he speaks, and that it is not the business of Revelation to rectify their opinions in such matters. Tindal made this rejoinder:

'Is there no difference between God's not rectifying men's sentiments in those matters and using himself such sentiments as needs be rectified; or between God's not mending men's logic and rhetoric where 'tis defective and using such himself; or between God's not contradicting vulgar notions and confirming them by speaking according to them. Can infinite wisdom despair of gaining or keeping people's affections without having recourse to such mean acts?'

He exposes with considerable effect the monstrosity of the doctrine of exclusive salvation. Must we not

consider, he asks, whether one can be said to be sent
as a Saviour of mankind, if he comes to shut Heaven's
gate against those to whom, before he came, it was
open provided they followed the dictates of their
reason? He criticizes the inconsistency of the impartial
and universal goodness of God, known to us by the
light of nature, with acts committed by Jehovah or his
prophets. Take the cases in which the order of nature
is violated to punish men for crimes of which they were
not guilty, such as Elijah's hindering rain from falling
for three years and a half. If God could break in upon
the ordinary rules of his providence to punish the
innocent for the guilty, we have no guarantee that if
he deals thus with us in this life, he will not act in
the same way in the life to come, 'since if the eternal
rules of justice are once broken how can we imagine
any stop?' But the ideals of holiness and justice in the
Old Testament are strange indeed. The holier men
are represented to be, the more cruel they seem and
the more addicted to cursing. How surprising to find
the holy prophet Elisha cursing in the name of the
Lord little children for calling him Bald-pate! And,
what is still more surprising, two she-bears immediately devoured forty-two little children.

I have remarked that theologians at this time
generally took the line of basing Christianity on reason
and not on faith. An interesting little book, *Christianity
not founded on Argument*, couched in the form of a
letter to a young gentleman at Oxford, by Henry
Dodwell (Junior) appeared in 1741, and pointed out
the dangers of such confidence in reason. It is an

ironical development of the principle of Bayle, working out the thesis that Christianity is essentially unreasonable, and that if you want to believe, reasoning is fatal. The cultivation of faith and reasoning produce contrary effects; the philosopher is disqualified for divine influences by his very progress in carnal wisdom; the Gospel must be received with all the obsequious submission of a babe who has no other disposition but to learn his lesson. Christ did not propose his doctrines to investigation; he did not lay the arguments for his mission before his disciples and give them time to consider calmly of their force, and liberty to determine as their reason should direct them; the apostles had no qualifications for the task, being the most artless and illiterate persons living. Dodwell exposes the absurdity of the Protestant position. To give all men liberty to judge for themselves and to expect at the same time that they shall be of the Preacher's mind is such a scheme for unanimity as one would scarcely imagine any one could be weak enough to devise in speculation and much less that any could ever be found hardy enough to avow and propose it to practice. The men of Rome 'shall rise up in the judgement (of all considering persons) against this generation and shall condemn it; for they invented but the one absurdity of infallibility, and behold a greater absurdity than infallibility is here'.

I have still to speak of the (Third) Earl of Shaftesbury, whose style has rescued his writings from entire neglect. His special interest was ethics. While the valuable work of most of the heterodox writers of this period lay in their destructive criticism of supernatural religion, they clung, as we have seen, to what was called natural religion—the belief in a kind and wise personal God, who created the world, governs it by natural laws, and desires our happiness. The idea was derived from ancient philosophers and had been revived by Lord Herbert of Cherbury in his Latin treatise *On Truth* (in the reign of James I). The deists contended that this was a sufficient basis for morality and that the Christian inducements to good behaviour were unnecessary. Shaftesbury in his *Inquiry concerning Virtue* (1699) debated the question and argued that the scheme of heaven and hell, with the selfish hopes and fears which they inspire, corrupts morality and that the only worthy motive for conduct is the beauty of virtue in itself. He does not even consider deism a necessary assumption for a moral code; he admits that the opinion of atheists does not undermine ethics. But he thinks that the belief in a good governor of the universe is a powerful support to the practice of virtue. He is a thorough optimist, and is perfectly satisfied with the admirable adaptation of means to ends, whereby it is the function of one animal to be food for another. He makes no attempt to reconcile the red claws and teeth of nature with the beneficence of its powerful artist. 'In the main all things are kindly and well disposed.' The atheist might have said that he preferred to be at the mercy of blind chance than in the hands of an autocrat who, if he pleased Lord Shaftesbury's sense of order, had created flies to be devoured by spiders. But this was an aspect of the universe which did not much trouble thinkers in the eighteenth century. On the other hand, the character of the God of the Old Testament roused Shaftesbury's aversion. He attacks Scripture not directly, but by allusion or with irony. He hints that if there is a God, he would be less displeased with atheists than with those who accepted him in the guise of Jehovah. As Plutarch said, 'I had rather men should say of me that there neither is nor ever was such a one as Plutarch, than they should say "There was a Plutarch, an unsteady, changeable, easily provokable and revengeful man."' Shaftesbury's significance is that he built up a positive theory of morals, and although it had no philosophical depth, his influence on French and German thinkers of the eighteenth century was immense.

In some ways perhaps the ablest of the deists, and certainly the most scholarly, was Rev. Conyers Middleton, who remained within the Church. He supported Christianity on grounds of utility. Even if it is an imposture, he said, it would be wrong to destroy it. For it is established by law and it has a long tradition behind it. Some traditional religion is necessary and it would be hopeless to supplant Christianity by reason. But his writings contain effective arguments which go to undermine Revelation. The most important was his *Free Inquiry* into Christian miracles (1748), which put in a new and dangerous light an old question: At what time did the Church cease to have the power of performing miracles? We shall see presently how Gibbon applied Middleton's method.

The leading adversaries of the deists appealed, like them, to reason, and, in appealing to reason, did much to undermine authority. The ablest defence of the faith, Bishop Butler's *Analogy* (1736), is suspected of having raised more doubts than it appeased. This was the experience of William Pitt the Younger, and the *Analogy* made James Mill (the utilitarian) an unbeliever. The deists argued that the unjust and cruel God of Revelation could not be the God of nature; Butler pointed to nature and said, There you behold cruelty and injustice. The argument was perfectly good against the optimism of Shaftesbury, but it plainly admitted of the conclusion—opposite to that which Butler wished to establish—that a just and beneficent God does not exist. Butler is driven to fall back on the sceptical argument that we are extremely ignorant; that all things are possible, even eternal hell fire; and that therefore the safe and prudent course is to accept the Christian doctrine. It may be remarked that this reasoning, with a few modifications, could be used in favour of other religions, at Mecca or at Timbuctoo. He has, in effect, revived the argument used by Pascal that if there is one chance in any very large number that Christianity is true, it is a man's interest to be a Christian; for, if it prove false, it will do him no harm to have believed it; if it prove true, he will be infinitely the gainer. Butler seeks indeed to show that the chances in favour amount to a probability, but his argument is essentially of the same intellectual and moral value as Pascal's. It has been pointed out that it leads by an easy logical step from the Anglican to the Roman

Church. Catholics and Protestants (as King Henry IV of France argued) agree that a Catholic may be saved; the Catholics assert that a Protestant will be damned; therefore the safe course is to embrace Catholicism.[1]

I have dwelt at some length upon some of the English deists, because, while they occupy an important place in the history of rationalism in England, they also supplied, along with Bayle, a great deal of the thought which, manipulated by brilliant writers on the other side of the Channel, captured the educated classes in France. We are now in the age of Voltaire. He was a convinced deist. He considered that the nature of the universe proved that it was made by a conscious architect, he held that God was required in the interests of conduct, and he ardently combated atheism. His great achievements were his efficacious labour in the cause of toleration, and his systematic warfare against superstitions. He was profoundly influenced by English thinkers, especially Locke and Bolingbroke. This statesman had concealed his infidelity during his lifetime except from his intimates; he had lived long as an exile in France; and his rationalistic essays were published (1754) after his death. Voltaire, whose literary genius converted the work of the English thinkers into a world-force, did not begin his campaign against Christianity till after the middle of the century, when superstitious practices and religious persecutions were becoming a scandal in his

[1] See Benn, *Rationalism in the Nineteenth Century*, vol. i, p. 138 *seq.*, for a good exposure of the fallacies and sophistries of Butler.

country.[1] He assailed the Catholic Church in every field with ridicule and satire. In a little work called *The Tomb of Fanaticism* (written 1736, published 1767), he begins by observing that a man who accepts his religion (as most people do) without examining it is like an ox which allows itself to be harnessed, and proceeds to review the difficulties in the Bible, the rise of Christianity, and the course of Church history; from which he concludes that every sensible man should hold the Christian sect in horror. 'Men are blind to prefer an absurd and sanguinary creed, supported by executioners and surrounded by fiery faggots, a creed which can only be approved by those to whom it gives power and riches, a particular creed only accepted in a small part of the world—to a simple and universal religion.' In the *Sermon of the Fifty* and the *Questions of Zapata* we can see what he owed to Bayle and English critics, but his touch is lighter and his irony more telling. His comment on geographical mistakes in the Old Testament is: 'God was evidently not strong in geography.' Having called attention to the 'horrible crime' of Lot's wife in looking backward, and her conversion into a pillar of salt, he hopes that the stories of Scripture will make us better, if they do not make us more enlightened. One of his favourite

---

[1]The scandals which Voltaire devoted himself to expose took place in the provinces and the victims were obscure persons. In Paris, the ideas of the sceptical philosophers were a fashionable interest and their persons were protected— unless the toes of some influential person were trodden on. Official repression was not so much lax as benevolent. See F. Brunetière, *Etudes critiques sur l'histoire de la littérature française*, 2me série, *La librairie sous Malesherbes*.—H.J.B.

methods is to approach Christian doctrines as a person who had just heard of the existence of Christians or Jews for the first time in his life.

His drama, *Saul* (1763), which the police tried to suppress, presents the career of David, the man after God's own heart, in all its naked horror. The scene in which Samuel reproves Saul for not having slain Agag will give an idea of the spirit of the piece.

SAMUEL: God commands me to tell you that he repents of having made you king.

SAUL: God repents! Only they who commit errors repent. His eternal wisdom cannot be unwise. God cannot commit errors.

SAMUEL: He can repent of having set on the throne those who do.

SAUL: Well, who does not? Tell me, what is my fault?

SAMUEL: You have pardoned a king.

AGAG: What! Is the fairest of virtues considered a crime in Judea?

SAMUEL (*to Agag*): Silence! do not blaspheme. (*To Saul*): Saul, formerly king of the Jews, did not God command you by my mouth to destroy all the Amalekites, without sparing women, or maidens, or children at the breast?

AGAG: Your god—gave such a command! You are mistaken, you meant to say, your devil.

SAMUEL: Saul, did you obey God?

SAUL: I did not suppose such a command was positive. I thought that goodness was the first attribute of the Supreme Being, and that a compassionate heart could not displease him.

SAMUEL: You are mistaken, unbeliever. God reproves you, your sceptre will pass into other hands.

Perhaps no writer has ever roused more hatred in Christendom than Voltaire. He was looked on as a sort of anti-Christ. That was natural; his attacks were so tremendously effective at the time. But he has been sometimes decried on the ground that he only demolished and made no effort to build up where he had pulled down. This is a narrow complaint. It might be replied that when a sewer is spreading plague in a town, we cannot wait to remove it till we have a new system of drains, and it may fairly be said that religion as practised in contemporary France was a poisonous sewer. But the true answer is that knowledge, and therefore civilization, are advanced by criticism and negation as well as by construction and positive discovery. When a man has the talent to attack with effect falsehood, prejudice, and imposture, it is his duty, if there are any social duties, to use it.

For constructive thinking we must go to the other great leader of French thought, Rousseau, who contributed to the growth of freedom in a different way. He was a deist, but his deism, unlike that of Voltaire, was religious and emotional. He regarded Christianity with a sort of reverent scepticism. But his thought was revolutionary and repugnant to orthodoxy; it made against authority in every sphere; and it had an enormous influence. The clergy perhaps dreaded his

theories more than the scoffs and negations of Voltaire.
For some years he was a fugitive on the face of the
earth. *Émile*, his brilliant contribution to the theory of
education, appeared in 1762. It contains some remarkable pages on religion, 'the profession of faith of a
Savoyard vicar', in which the author's deistic faith is
strongly affirmed and revelation and theology rejected.
The book was publicly burned in Paris and an order
issued for Rousseau's arrest. Forced by his friends to
flee, he was debarred from returning to Geneva, for
the government of that canton followed the example
of Paris. He sought refuge in the canton of Bern and
was ordered to quit. He then fled to the principality of
Neufchâtel which belonged to Prussia. Frederick the
Great, the one really tolerant ruler of the age, gave him
protection, but he was persecuted and calumniated
by the local clergy, who but for Frederick would have
expelled him, and he went to England for a few months
(1766), then returning to France, where he was left
unmolested till his death. The religious views of
Rousseau are only a minor point in his heretical speculations. It was by his daring social and political theories
that he set the world on fire. His *Social Contract* in
which these theories were set forth was burned at
Geneva. Though his principles will not stand criticism
for a moment, and though his doctrine worked mis-
chief by its extraordinary power of turning men into
fanatics, yet it contributed to progress, by helping to
discredit privilege and to establish the view that the
object of a State is to secure the wellbeing of *all* its
members.

Deism—whether in the semi-Christian form of Rousseau or the anti-Christian form of Voltaire—was a house built on the sand, and thinkers arose in France, England, and Germany to shatter its foundations. In France, it proved to be only a halfway inn to atheism. In 1770, French readers were startled by the appearance of Baron D'Holbach's *System of Nature*, in which God's existence and the immortality of the soul were denied and the world declared to be matter spontaneously moving.

Holbach was a friend of Diderot, who had also come to reject deism. All the leading ideas in the revolt against the Church had a place in Diderot's great work, the *Encyclopaedia*, in which a number of leading thinkers collaborated with him. It was not merely a scientific book of reference. It was representative of the whole movement of the enemies of faith. It was intended to lead men from Christianity with its original sin to a new conception of the world as a place which can be made agreeable and in which the actual evils are due not to radical faults of human nature but to perverse institutions and perverse education. To divert interest from the dogmas of religion to the improvement of society, to persuade the world that man's felicity depends not on Revelation but on social transformation—this was what Diderot and Rousseau in their different ways did so much to effect. And their work influenced those who did not abandon orthodoxy; it affected the spirit of the Church itself. Contrast the Catholic Church in France in the eighteenth, and in the nineteenth century. Without the work of Voltaire, Rousseau, Diderot, and their fellow-combatants, would it have been reformed? 'The Christian Churches' (I quote Lord Morley) 'are assimilating as rapidly as their formulae will permit the new light and the more generous moral ideas and the higher spirituality of teachers who have abandoned all churches and who are systematically denounced as enemies of the souls of men.'

In England the prevalent deistic thought did not lead to the same intellectual consequences as in France; yet Hume, the greatest English philosopher of the century, showed that the arguments commonly adduced for a personal God were untenable. I may first speak of his discussion on miracles in his *Essay on Miracles* and in his philosophical *Inquiry concerning Human Understanding* (1748). Hitherto the credibility of miracles had not been submitted to a general examination independent of theological assumptions. Hume, pointing out that there must be a uniform experience against every miraculous event (otherwise it would not merit the name of miracle), and that it will require stronger testimony to establish a miracle than an event which is not contrary to experience, lays down the general maxim that 'no testimony is sufficient to establish a miracle unless the testimony is of such a kind that its falsehood would be more miraculous than the fact which it endeavours to establish'. But, as a matter of fact, no testimony exists of which the falsehood would be a prodigy. We cannot find in history any miracle attested by a sufficient number of men of such unquestionable good sense, education and learning, as to secure us against all delusion in themselves; of such undoubted integrity as to place them beyond all suspicion of any design to deceive others; of such credit in the eyes of mankind as to have a great deal to lose in case of their being detected in any falsehood, and at the same time attesting facts performed in such a public manner as to · render detection unavoidable—all which circumstances are requisite to give us a full assurance in the testimony of men.

In the *Dialogues on Natural Religion* which were not published till after his death (1776), Hume made an attack on the 'argument from design', on which deists and Christians alike relied to prove the existence of a Deity. The argument is that the world presents clear marks of design, endless adaptation of means to ends, which can only be explained as due to the deliberate plan of a powerful intelligence. Hume disputes the inference on the ground that a mere intelligent being is not a sufficient cause to explain the effect. For the argument must be that the system of the material world demands as a cause a corresponding system of interconnected ideas; but such a mental system would demand an explanation of *its* existence just as much as the material world; and thus we find ourselves committed to an endless series of causes. But in any case, even if the argument held, it would prove only the existence of a Deity whose powers, though superior to man's, might be very limited and whose workmanship might be very imperfect. For this world may be very faulty, compared to a superior standard. It may be the first rude experiment 'of some infant Deity who afterwards abandoned it, ashamed of his lame performance'; or the work of some inferior Deity at which his superior would scoff; or the production of some old superannuated Deity which since his death has pursued an adventurous career from the first impulse which he gave it. An argument which leaves such deities in the running is worse than useless for the purposes of Deism or of Christianity.

The sceptical philosophy of Hume had less influence on the general public than Gibbon's *Decline and Fall of the Roman Empire*. Of the numerous freethinking books that appeared in England in the eighteenth century, this is the only one which is still a widely read classic. In what a lady friend of Dr. Johnson called 'the two offensive chapters' (XV and XVI) the causes of the rise and success of Christianity are for the first time critically investigated as a simple historical phenomenon. Like most freethinkers of the time Gibbon thought it well to protect himself and his work against the possibility of prosecution by paying ironical lip-homage to the orthodox creed. But even if there had been no such danger, he could not have chosen a more incisive weapon for his merciless criticism of orthodox opinion than the irony which he wielded with superb ease. Having pointed out that the victory of Christianity is obviously and satisfactorily explained by the convincing evidence of the doctrine and by the ruling providence of its great Author, he proceeds 'with becoming submission' to inquire into the secondary causes. He traces the history of the faith up to the time of Constantine in such a way as clearly to suggest that the hypothesis of divine inter-position is superfluous and that we have to do with a purely human development. He marshals, with ironical protests, the obvious objections to the alleged evidence for supernatural control. He does not himself criticize Moses and the prophets, but he reproduces the objec-tions which were made against their authority by 'the vain science of the gnostics'. He notes that the doctrine of immortality is omitted in the law of Moses, but this doubtless was a mysterious dispensation of Providence. We cannot entirely remove 'the imputation of ignor-ance and obscurity which has been so arrogantly cast on the first proselytes of Christianity', but we must 'convert the occasion of scandal into a subject of edification' and remember that 'the lower we depress the temporal condition of the first Christians, the more reason we shall find to admire their merit and success'.

Gibbon's treatment of miracles from the purely historical point of view (he owed a great deal to Middleton, see above, p. 119) was particularly dis-concerting. In the early age of Christianity 'the laws of nature were frequently suspended for the benefit of the Church. But the sages of Greece and Rome turned aside from the awful spectacle, and, pursuing the ordinary occupations of life and study, appeared unconscious of any alterations in the moral or physical government of the world. Under the reign of Tiberius, the whole earth, or at least a celebrated province of the Roman Empire, was involved in a praeternatural darkness of three hours. Even this miraculous event, which ought to have excited the wonder, the curiosity, and the devotion of mankind, passed without notice in an age of science and history. It happened during the lifetime of Seneca and the elder Pliny, who must have experienced the immediate effects, or received the earliest intelligence, of the prodigy. Each of these philosophers in a laborious work has recorded all the great phenomena of nature, earthquakes, meteors, comets, and eclipses, which his indefatigable curiosity could collect. Both the one and the other have omitted to mention the greatest phenomenon to which the mortal eye has been witness since the creation of the globe.' How 'shall we excuse the supine inattention of the pagan and philosophic world to those evidences which were presented by the hand of Omnipotence, not to their reason, but to their senses'?

Again, if every believer is convinced of the reality of miracles, every reasonable man is convinced of their cessation. Yet every age bears testimony to miracles, and the testimony seems no less respectable than that of the preceding generation. When did they cease? How was it that the generation which saw the last genuine miracles performed could not distinguish them from the impostures which followed? Had men so soon forgotten 'the style of the divine artist'? The inference is that genuine and spurious miracles are indistinguishable. But the credulity or 'softness of temper' among early believers was beneficial to the cause of truth and religion. 'In modern times, a latent and even involuntary scepticism adheres to the most pious dispositions. Their admission of supernatural truths is much less an active consent than a cold and passive acquiescence. Accustomed long since to observe and to respect the invariable order of nature, our reason, or at least our imagination, is not sufficiently prepared to sustain the visible action of the Deity.'

Gibbon had not the advantage of the minute critical labours which in the following century were expended on his sources of information, but his masterly exposure of the conventional history of the early Church remains in many of its most important points perfectly valid to-day. I suspect that his artillery has produced more effect on intelligent minds in subsequent generations than the archery of Voltaire. For his book became indispensable as the great history of the Middle Ages; the most orthodox could not do without it; and the poison must have often worked.

We have seen how theological controversy in the first half of the eighteenth century had turned on the question whether the revealed religion was consistent and compatible with natural religion. The deistic attacks, on this line, were almost exhausted by the middle of the century, and the orthodox thought that they had been satisfactorily answered. But it was not enough to show that the revelation is reasonable; it was necessary to prove that it is real and rests on a solid historical basis. This was the question raised in an acute form by the criticisms of Hume and Middleton (1748) on miracles. The ablest answer was given by Paley in his *Evidences of Christianity* (1794), the only one of the apologies of that age which is still read, though it has ceased to have any value. Paley's theology illustrates how orthodox opinions are coloured, unconsciously, by the spirit of the time. He proved (in his *Natural Theology*) the existence of God by the argument from design—without taking any account of the criticisms of Hume on that argument. Just as a watchmaker is inferred from a watch, so a divine workman is inferred from contrivances in nature. Paley takes his instances of such contrivance largely from the organs and constitution of the human body. His idea of God is that of an ingenious contriver dealing with rather obstinate material. Paley's 'God' (Leslie Stephen remarked) 'has been civilized like man; he has become scientific and ingenious; he is superior to Watt or Priestley in devising mechanical and chemical contrivances, and is therefore made in the image of that generation of which Watt and Priestley were conspicuous lights.' When a God of this kind is established there is no difficulty about miracles, and it is on miracles that Paley bases the case for Christianity—all other arguments are subsidiary. And his proof of the New Testament miracles is that the apostles who were eye-witnesses believed in them, for otherwise they would not have acted and suffered in the cause of their new religion. Paley's defence is the performance of an able legal adviser to the Almighty.

The list of the English deistic writers of the eighteenth century closes with one whose name is more familiar than any of his predecessors, Thomas Paine. A Norfolk man, he migrated to America and played a leading part in the Revolution. Then he returned to England and in 1791 published his *Rights of Man* in two parts. I have been considering, almost exclusively, freedom of thought in religion, because it may be taken as the thermometer for freedom of thought in general. At this period it was as dangerous to publish revolutionary opinions in politics as in theology. Paine was an enthusiastic admirer of the American Constitution and a supporter of the French Revolution (in which also he was to play a part). His *Rights of Man* is an indictment of the monarchical form of government and a plea for representative democracy. It had an enormous sale, a cheap edition was issued, and the government, finding that it was accessible to the poorer classes, decided to prosecute. Paine escaped to France, and received a brilliant ovation at Calais, which returned him as deputy to the National Convention. His trial for high treason came on at the end of 1792. Among the passages in his book, on which the charge was founded were these: 'All hereditary government is in its nature tyranny.' 'The time is not very distant when England will laugh at itself for sending to Holland, Hanover, Zell, or Brunswick, for men [meaning King William III, and King George I] at the expense of a million a year who understood neither her laws, her language nor her interest, and whose capacities would scarcely have fitted them for the office of a parish constable. If government could be trusted to such hands, it must be some easy and simple thing indeed, and materials fit for all the purposes may be found in every town and village in England.' Erskine was Paine's counsel and he made a fine oration in defence of freedom of speech.

'Constraint', he said, 'is the natural parent of resistance, and a pregnant proof that reason is not on the side of those who use it. You must all remember, gentlemen, Lucian's pleasant story: Jupiter and a countryman were walking together, conversing with great freedom and familiarity upon the subject of heaven and earth. The countryman listened with attention and acquiescence while Jupiter strove only to convince him; but happening to hint a doubt, Jupiter turned hastily around and threatened him with his thunder. "Ah, ha!" says the countryman, "now Jupiter, I know that you are wrong: you are always wrong when you appeal to your thunder." This is the case with me. I can reason with the people of England, but I cannot fight against the thunder of authority.'

Paine was found guilty and outlawed. He soon committed a new offence by the publication of an anti-Christian work, *The Age of Reason* (1794 and 1796), which he began to write in the Paris prison into which he had been thrown by Robespierre. This book is remarkable as the first important English publication in which the Christian scheme of salvation and the Bible are assailed in plain language without any disguise or reserve. In the second place it was written in such a way as to reach the masses. And, thirdly, while the criticisms on the Bible are in the same vein as those of the earlier deists, Paine is the first to present with force the incongruity of the Christian scheme with the conception of the universe attained by astronomical science.

"Though it is not a direct article of the Christian

system that this world that we inhabit is the whole of the inhabitable globe, yet it is so worked up therewith—from what is called the Mosaic account of the creation, the story of Eve and the apple, and the counterpart of that story, the death of the Son of God —that to believe otherwise (that is, to believe that God created a plurality of worlds at least as numerous as what we call stars) renders the Christian system of faith at once little and ridiculous, and scatters it in the mind like feathers in the air. The two beliefs cannot be held together in the same mind; and he who thinks that he believes both has thought but little of either.'

As an ardent deist, who regarded nature as God's revelation, Paine was able to press this argument with particular force. Referring to some of the tales in the Old Testament, he says: 'When we contemplate the immensity of that Being who directs and governs the incomprehensible *Whole*, of which the utmost ken of human sight can discover but a part, we ought to feel shame at calling such paltry stories the Word of God.'

The book drew a reply from Bishop Watson, one of those admirable eighteenth-century divines, who admitted the right of private judgement and thought that argument should be met by argument and not by force. His reply had the rather significant title, *An Apology for the Bible*. George III remarked that he was not aware that any apology was needed for that book. It is a weak defence, but is remarkable for the concessions which it makes to several of Paine's criticisms of

Scripture—admissions which were calculated to damage the doctrine of the infallibility of the Bible.

It was doubtless in consequence of the enormous circulation of the *Age of Reason* that a Society for the Suppression of Vice decided to prosecute the publisher. Unbelief was common among the ruling class, but the view was firmly held that religion was necessary for the populace and that any attempt to disseminate unbelief among the lower classes must be suppressed. Religion was regarded as a valuable instrument to keep the poor in order. It is notable that of the earlier rationalists (apart from the case of Woolston) the only one who was punished was Peter Annet a schoolmaster, who tried to popularize freethought and was sentenced for diffusing 'diabolical' opinions to the pillory and hard labour (1763). Paine held that the people at large had the right of access to all new ideas, and he wrote so as to reach the people. Hence his book must be suppressed. At the trial (1797) the judge placed every obstacle in the way of the defence. The publisher was sentenced to a year's imprisonment.

This was not the end of Paine prosecutions. In 1811 a Third Part of the *Age of Reason* appeared, and Eaton the publisher was condemned to eighteen months' imprisonment and to stand in the pillory once a month. The judge, Lord Ellenborough, said in his charge, that 'to deny the truths of the book which is the foundation of our faith has never been permitted'. The poet Shelley addressed to Lord Ellenborough a scathing letter. 'Do you think to convert Mr. Eaton to your religion by embittering his existence? You might force him by torture to profess your tenets, but he could not believe them except you should make them credible, which perhaps exceeds your power. Do you think to please the God you worship by this exhibition of your zeal? If so, the demon to whom some nations offer human hecatombs is less barbarous than the deity of civilized society!' In 1819 Richard Carlisle was prosecuted for publishing the *Age of Reason* and sentenced to a large fine and three years' imprisonment. Unable to pay the fine he was kept in prison for three years. His wife and sister, who carried on the business and continued to sell the book, were fined and imprisoned soon afterwards and a whole host of shop assistants.

If his publishers suffered in England, the author himself suffered in America where bigotry did all it could to make the last years of his life bitter.

The age of enlightenment began in Germany in the middle of the eighteenth century. In most of the German States, thought was considerably less free than in England. Under Frederick the Great's father, the philosopher Wolff was banished from Prussia for according to the moral teachings of the Chinese sage Confucius a praise which, it was thought, ought to be reserved for Christianity. He returned after the accession of Frederick, under whose tolerant rule Prussia was an asylum for those writers who suffered for their opinions in neighbouring States. Frederick, indeed, held the view which was held by so many English rationalists of the time, and is still held widely enough, that freethought is not desirable for the multitude, because they are incapable of understanding philosophy. Germany felt the influence of the English deists, of the French freethinkers, and of Spinoza; but in the German rationalistic propaganda of this period there is nothing very original or interesting. The names of Edelmann and Bahrdt may be mentioned. The works of Edelmann, who attacked the inspiration of the Bible, were burned in various cities, and he was forced to seek Frederick's protection at Berlin. Bahrdt was more aggressive than any other writer of the time. Originally a preacher, it was by slow degrees that he moved away from the orthodox faith. His translation of the New Testament cut short his ecclesiastical career. His last years were spent as an inn-keeper. His writings, for instance his popular *Letters on the Bible*, must have had a considerable effect, if we may judge by the hatred which he excited among theologians.

It was not, however, in direct rationalistic propaganda, but in literature and philosophy that the German enlightenment of this century expressed itself. The most illustrious men of letters, Goethe (who was profoundly influenced by Spinoza) and Schiller, stood outside the Churches, and the effect of their writings and of the whole literary movement of the time made for the freest treatment of human experience.

One German thinker shook the world—the philosopher Kant. His *Critic of Pure Reason* demonstrated that when we attempt to prove by the light of the intellect the existence of God and the immortality of the Soul, we fall helplessly into contradictions. His destructive criticism of the argument from design and all natural theology was more complete than that of Hume; and his philosophy, different though his system was, issued in the same practical result as that of Locke, to confine knowledge to experience. It is true that afterwards, in the interest of ethics, he tried to smuggle in by a back-door the Deity whom he had turned out by the front gate, but the attempt was not a success. His philosophy—while it led to new speculative systems in which the name of God was used to mean something very different from the deistic conception— was a significant step further in the deliverance of reason from the yoke of authority.

Chapter VII

THE PROGRESS OF RATIONALISM: NINETEENTH CENTURY

MODERN science, heralded by the researches of Copernicus, was founded in the seventeenth century, which saw the demonstration of the Copernican theory, the discovery of gravitation, the discovery of the circulation of the blood, and the foundation of modern chemistry and physics. The true nature of comets was ascertained and they ceased to be regarded as signs of heavenly wrath. But several generations were to pass before science became, in Protestant countries, an involuntary arch-enemy of theology. Till the nineteenth century, it was only in minor points, such as the movement of the earth, that proved scientific facts seemed to conflict with Scripture, and it was easy enough to explain away these inconsistencies by a new interpretation of the sacred texts. Yet remarkable facts were accumulating which, though not explained by science, seemed to menace the credibility of Biblical history. If the story of Noah's Ark and the Flood is true, how was it that beasts unable to swim or fly inhabit America and the islands of the Ocean? And what about the new species which were constantly being found in the New World and did not exist in the Old? Where did the kangaroos of Australia drop from? The only explanation compatible with received theology seemed to be the hypothesis of innumerable new

acts of creation, later than the Flood. It was in the
field of natural history that scientific men of the
eighteenth century suffered most from the coercion of
authority. Linnaeus felt it in Sweden, Buffon in France.
Buffon was compelled to retract hypotheses which he
put forward about the formation of the earth in his
Natural History (1749), and to state that he believed
implicitly in the Bible account of Creation.

At the beginning of the nineteenth century Laplace
worked out the mechanics of the universe, on the
nebular hypothesis. His results dispensed, as he said
to Napoleon, with the hypothesis of God, and were
duly denounced. His theory involved a long physical
process before the earth and solar system came to be
formed; but this was not fatal, for a little ingenuity
might preserve the credit of the first chapter of Genesis.
Geology was to prove a more formidable enemy to the
Biblical story of the Creation and the Deluge. The
theory of a French naturalist (Cuvier) that the earth
had repeatedly experienced catastrophes, each of
which necessitated a new creative act, helped for a
time to save the belief in divine intervention, and Lyell,
in his *Principles of Geology* (1830), while he undermined
the assumption of catastrophes by showing that the
earth's history could be explained by the ordinary
processes which we still see in operation, yet held
fast to successive acts of creation. It was not till 1863
that he presented fully, in his *Antiquity of Man*, the
evidence which showed that the human race had
inhabited the earth for a far longer period than could
be reconciled with the record of Scripture. That

record might be adapted to the results of science in
regard not only to the earth itself but also to the plants
and lower animals, by explaining the word 'day' in the
Jewish story of creation to signify some long period
of time. But this way out was impossible in the case
of the creation of man, for the sacred chronology is
quite definite. An English divine of the seventeenth
century ingeniously calculated that man was created
by the Trinity on 23rd October, B.C. 4004, at 9 o'clock
in the morning, and no reckoning of the Bible dates
could put the event much further back. Other evidence
reinforced the conclusions from geology, but geology
alone was sufficient to damage irretrievably the historical truth of the Jewish legend of Creation. The
only means of rescuing it was to suppose that God
had created misleading evidence for the express purpose
of deceiving man.

Geology shook the infallibility of the Bible, but left
the creation of some prehistoric Adam and Eve a still
admissible hypothesis. Here however zoology stepped
in, and pronounced upon the origin of man. It was an
old conjecture that the higher forms of life, including
man, had developed out of lower forms, and advanced
thinkers had been reaching the conclusion that the
universe, as we find it, is the result of a continuous
process, unbroken by supernatural interference, and
explicable by uniform natural laws. But while the
reign of law in the world of non-living matter seemed
to be established, the world of life could be considered
a field in which the theory of divine intervention is
perfectly valid, so long as science failed to assign

satisfactory causes for the origination of the various
kinds of animals and plants. The publication of
Darwin's *Origin of Species* in 1859 is, therefore, a
landmark not only in science but in the war between
science and theology. When this book appeared, Bishop
Wilberforce truly said that 'the principle of natural
selection is incompatible with the word of God', and
theologians in Germany and France as well as in
England cried aloud against the threatened dethrone-
ment of the Deity. The appearance of the *Descent of
Man* (1871), in which the evidence for the pedigree of
the human race from lower animals was marshalled
with masterly force, renewed the outcry. The Bible
said that God created man in his own image, Darwin
said that man descended from an ape. The feelings of
the orthodox world may be expressed in the words of
Gladstone: 'Upon the grounds of what is called
evolution God is relieved of the labour of creation,
and in the name of unchangeable laws is discharged
from governing the world.' It was a discharge which,
as Spencer observed, had begun with Newton's discovery of gravitation. If Darwin did not, as is now
recognized, supply a complete explanation of the
origin of species, his researches shattered the supernatural theory and confirmed the view to which many
able thinkers had been led that development is continuous
in the living as in the non-living world. Another nail
was driven into the coffin of Creation and the Fall
of Adam, and the doctrine of redemption could only
be rescued by making it independent of the Jewish
fable on which it was founded.

Darwinism, as it is called, has had the larger effect of discrediting the theory of the adaptation of means to ends in nature by an external and infinitely powerful intelligence. The inadequacy of the argument from design, as a proof of God's existence, had been shown by the logic of Hume and Kant; but the observation of the life-processes of nature shows that the very analogy between nature and art, on which the argument depends, breaks down. The impropriety of the analogy has been pointed out, in a telling way, by a German writer (Lange). If a man wants to shoot a hare which is in a certain field, he does not procure thousands of guns, surround the field, and cause them all to be fired off; or if he wants a house to live in, he does not build a whole town and abandon to weather and decay all the houses but one. If he did either of these things we should say he was mad or amazingly unintelligent; his actions certainly would not be held to indicate a powerful mind, expert in adapting means to ends. But these are the sort of things that nature does. Her wastefulness in the propagation of life is reckless. For the production of one life she sacrifices innumerable germs. The 'end' is achieved in one case out of thousands; the rule is destruction and failure. If intelligence had anything to do with this bungling process, it would be an intelligence infinitely low. And the finished product, if regarded as a work of design, points to incompetence in the designer. Take the human eye. An illustrious man of science (Helmholtz) said, 'If an optician sent it to me as an instrument, I should send it back with reproaches for the carelessness of his work

and demand the return of my money.' Darwin showed
how the phenomena might be explained as events not
brought about intentionally, but due to exceptional
concurrences of circumstances.

The phenomena of nature are a system of things
which co-exist and follow each other according to
invariable laws. This deadly proposition was asserted
early in the nineteenth century to be an axiom of
science. It was formulated by Mill (in his *System of
Logic*, 1843) as the foundation on which scientific
induction rests. It means that at any moment the state
of the whole universe is the effect of its state at the
preceding moment; the causal sequence between two
successive states is not broken by any arbitrary interference suppressing or altering the relation between
cause and effect. Some ancient Greek philosophers
were convinced of this principle; the work done by
modern science in every field seems to be a verification
of it. But it need not be stated in such an absolute
form. Recently, scientific men have been inclined to
express the axiom with more reserve and less dogma-
tically. They are prepared to recognize that it is simply
a postulate without which the scientific comprehension
of the universe would be impossible, and they are
inclined to state it not as a law of causation—for the
idea of causation leads into metaphysics—but rather
as uniformity of experience. But they are not readier
to admit exceptions to this uniformity than their predecessors were to admit exceptions to the law of causation.

The idea of development has been applied not only
to nature, but to the mind of man and to the history

of civilization, including thought and religion. The first who attempted to apply this idea methodically to the whole universe was not a student of natural science, but a metaphysician, Hegel. His extremely difficult philosophy had such a wide influence on thought that a few words must be said about its tendency. He conceived the whole of existence as what he called the Absolute Idea, which is not in space or time and is compelled by the laws of its being to manifest itself in the process of the world, first externalizing itself in nature, and then becoming conscious of itself as spirit in individual minds. His system is hence called Absolute Idealism. The attraction which it exercised has probably been in great measure due to the fact that it was in harmony with nineteenth century thought, in so far as it conceived the process of the world, both in nature and spirit, as a necessary development from lower to higher stages. In this respect indeed Hegel's vision was limited. He treats the process as if it were practically complete already, and does not take into account the probability of further development in the future, to which other thinkers of his own time were turning their attention. But what concerns us here is that, while Hegel's system is 'idealistic', finding the explanation of the universe in thought and not in matter, it tended as powerfully as any materialistic system to subvert orthodox beliefs. It is true that some have claimed it as supporting Christianity. A certain colour is lent to this by Hegel's view that the Christian creed, as the highest religion, contains doctrines which express imperfectly some of the ideas of the highest philosophy—his own; along with the fact that he sometimes speaks of the Absolute Idea as if it were a person, though personality would be a limitation inconsistent with his conception of it. But it is sufficient to observe that, whatever value he assigned to Christianity, he regarded it from the *superior* standpoint of a purely intellectual philosophy, not as a special revelation of truth, but as a certain approximation to the truth which philosophy alone can reach; and it may be said with some confidence that any one who comes under Hegel's spell feels that he is in possession of a theory of the universe which relieves him from the need or desire of any revealed religion. His influence in Germany, Russia, and elsewhere has entirely made for highly unorthodox thought.

Hegel was not aggressive, he was superior. His French contemporary, Comte, who also thought out a comprehensive system, aggressively and explicitly rejected theology as an obsolete way of explaining the universe. He rejected metaphysics likewise, and all that Hegel stood for, as equally useless, on the ground that metaphysicians explain nothing, but merely describe phenomena in abstract terms, and that questions about the origin of the world and why it exists are quite beyond the reach of reason. Both theology and metaphysics are superseded by science—the investigation of causes and effects and co-existences; and the future progress of society will be guided by the scientific view of the world which confines itself to the positive data of experience. Comte was convinced that religion is a social necessity, and, to supply the place of the theological religions which he pronounced to be doomed, he invented a new religion—the religion of Humanity. It differs from the great religions of the world in having no supernatural or non-rational articles of belief, and on that account he had few adherents. But the *Positive Philosophy* of Comte has exercised great influence, not least in England, where its principles have been promulgated especially by Frederic Harrison, who in the latter half of the nineteenth century has been one of the most indefatigable workers in the cause of reason against authority.

Another comprehensive system was worked out by an Englishman, Herbert Spencer. Like Comte's, it was based on science, and attempts to show how, starting with a nebular universe, the whole knowable world, psychical and social as well as physical, can be deduced. His *Synthetic Philosophy* perhaps did more than anything else to make the idea of evolution familiar in England.

I must mention one other modern explanation of the world, that of Haeckel, the zoologist, professor at Jena, who may be called the prophet of evolution. His *Creation of Man* (1868) covered the same ground as Darwin's *Descent*, had an enormous circulation, and was translated, I believe, into fourteen languages. His *World-riddles* (1899) enjoys the same popularity. He has taught, like Spencer, that the principle of evolution applies not only to the history of nature, but also to human civilization and human thought. He differs from Spencer and Comte in not assuming any unknowable reality behind natural phenomena. His adversaries commonly stigmatize his theory as materialism, but this is a mistake. Like Spinoza he recognizes matter and mind, body and thought, as two inseparable sides of ultimate reality, which he calls God; in fact, he identifies his philosophy with that of Spinoza. And he logically proceeds to conceive material atoms as thinking. His idea of the physical world is based on the old mechanical conception of matter, which in recent years has been discredited. But Haeckel's *Monism*,[1] as he called his doctrine, has lately been reshaped and in its new form promises to exercise wide influence on thoughtful people in Germany. I will return later to this Monistic movement.

It had been a fundamental principle of Comte that human actions and human history are as strictly subject as nature is, to the law of causation. Two psychological works appeared in England in 1855 (Bain's *Senses and Intellect* and Spencer's *Principles of Psychology*), which taught that our volitions are completely determined, being the inevitable consequences of chains of causes and effects. But a far deeper impression was produced two years later by the first volume of Buckle's *History of Civilization in England* (a work of much less permanent value), which attempted to apply this principle to history. Men act in consequence of motives; their motives are the results of preceding facts; so that 'if we were acquainted with the whole of the antecedents and with all the laws of their movements, we could with unerring certainty predict the whole of their immediate results'. Thus

[1] From Greek *monos*, alone.

history is an unbroken chain of causes and effects. Chance is excluded; it is a mere name for the defects of our knowledge. Mysterious and providential interference is excluded. Buckle maintained God's existence, but eliminated him from history; and his book dealt a resounding blow at the theory that human actions are not submitted to the law of universal causation.

The science of anthropology has in recent years aroused wide interest. Inquiries into the condition of early man have shown (independently of Darwinism) that there is nothing to be said for the view that he fell from a higher to a lower state; the evidence points to a slow rise from mere animality. The origin of religious beliefs has been investigated, with results disquieting for orthodoxy. The researches of students of anthropology and comparative religion—such as Tylor, Robertson Smith, and Frazer—have gone to show that mysterious ideas and dogmas and rites which were held to be peculiar to the Christian revelation are analogous to crude ideas of primitive religions. That the mystery of the Eucharist may be compared to the heathen rite of eating a dead god, that the death and resurrection of a god in human form, which form the central fact of Christianity, and the miraculous birth of a Saviour are features which it has in common with pagan religions—such conclusions are supremely unedifying. It may be said that in themselves they are not fatal to the claims of the current theology. It may be held, for instance, that, as part of Christian revelation, such ideas acquired a new significance and that God wisely availed himself of familiar beliefs—which, though false and leading to cruel practices, he himself had undeniably permitted—in order to construct a scheme of redemption which should appeal to the prejudices of man. Some minds may find satisfaction in this sort of explanation, but it may be suspected that most of the few who study modern researches into the origin of religious beliefs will feel the lines which were supposed to mark off the Christian from all other faiths dissolving before their eyes.

The general result of the advance of science, including anthropology, has been to create a coherent view of the world, in which the Christian scheme, based on the notions of an unscientific age and on the arrogant assumption that the universe was made for man, has no suitable or reasonable place. If Paine felt this a hundred years ago, it is far more apparent now. All minds however are not equally impressed with this incongruity. There are many who will admit the proofs furnished by science that the biblical record as to the antiquity of man is false, but are not affected by the incongruity between the scientific and theological conceptions of the world.

For such minds science has only succeeded in carrying some entrenchments, which may be abandoned without much harm. It has made the old orthodox view of the infallibility of the Bible untenable, and upset the doctrine of the Creation and Fall. But it would still be possible for Christianity to maintain the supernatural claim, by modifying its theory of the authority of the Bible and revising its theory of redemption, if the evidence of natural science were the only group of facts with which it collided. It might be argued that the law of universal causation is a hypothesis inferred from experience, but that experience includes the testimonies of history and must therefore take account of the clear evidence of miraculous occurrences in the New Testament (evidence which is valid, even if that book was not inspired). Thus, a stand could be taken against the generalization of science on the firm ground of historical fact. That solid ground, however, has given way, undermined by historical criticism, which has been more deadly than the common-sense criticism of the eighteenth century.

The methodical examination of the records contained in the Bible, dealing with them as if they were purely human documents, is the work of the nineteenth century. Something, indeed, had already been done. Spinoza, for instance (above, p. 110), and Simon, a Frenchman whose books were burnt, were pioneers; and the modern criticism of the Old Testament was begun by Astruc (professor of medicine at Paris), who discovered an important clue for distinguishing different documents used by the compiler of the Book of Genesis (1753). His German contemporary, Reimarus, a student of the New Testament, anticipated the modern conclusion that Jesus had no intention of founding a new religion, and saw that the Gospel of St. John presents a different figure from the Jesus of the other evangelists.

But in the nineteenth century the methods of criticism, applied by German scholars to Homer and

to the records of early Roman history, were extended
to the investigation of the Bible. The work has been
done principally in Germany. The old tradition that
the Pentateuch was written by Moses has been completely discredited. It is now agreed unanimously
by all who have studied the facts that the Pentateuch
was put together from a number of different documents
of different ages, the earliest dating from the ninth,
the last from the fifth, century B.C.; and there are
later minor additions. An important, though un-
designed, contribution was made to this exposure by
an Englishman, Colenso, Bishop of Natal. It had been
held that the oldest of the documents which had been
distinguished was a narrative which begins in Genesis,
Chapter I, but there was the difficulty that this narrative
seemed to be closely associated with the legislation of
Leviticus which could be proved to belong to the fifth
century. In 1862 Colenso published the first part of
his *Pentateuch and the Book of Joshua Critically
Examined*. His doubts of the truth of Old Testament
history had been awakened by a converted Zulu who
asked the intelligent question whether he could really
believe in the story of the Flood, 'that all the beasts and
birds and creeping things upon the earth, large and
small, from hot countries and cold, came thus by pairs
and entered into the ark with Noah? And did Noah
gather food for them *all*, for the beasts and birds of
prey as well as the rest?' The bishop then proceeded to
test the accuracy of the inspired books by examining
the numerical statements which they contain. The
results were fatal to them as historical records. Quite

apart from miracles (the possibility of which he did not question), he showed that the whole story of the sojourn of the Israelites in Egypt and the wilderness was full of absurdities and impossibilities. Colenso's book raised a storm of indignation in England—he was known as 'the wicked bishop'; but on the Continent its reception was very different. The portions of the Pentateuch and Joshua, which he proved to be unhistorical, belonged precisely to the narrative which had caused perplexity; and critics were led by his results to conclude that, like the Levitical laws with which it was connected, it was as late as the fifth century.

One of the most striking results of the researches on the Old Testament has been that the Jews themselves handled their traditions freely. Each of the successive documents, which were afterwards woven together, was written by men who adopted a perfectly free attitude towards the older traditions, and having no suspicion that they were of divine origin did not bow down before their authority. It was reserved for the Christians to invest with infallible authority the whole indiscriminate lump of these Jewish documents, inconsistent not only in their tendencies (since they reflect the spirit of different ages), but also in some respects in substance. The examination of most of the other Old Testament books has led to conclusions likewise adverse to the orthodox view of their origin and character. New knowledge on many points has been derived from the Babylonian literature which has been recovered during the last half century. One of the earliest (1872) and most sensational discoveries was that the Jews got their story of the Flood from Babylonian mythology.

Modern criticism of the New Testament began with the stimulating works of Baur and of Strauss, whose *Life of Jesus* (1835), in which the supernatural was entirely rejected, had an immense success and caused furious controversy. Both these' rationalists were influenced by Hegel. At the same time a classical scholar, Lachmann, laid the foundations of the criticism of the Greek text of the New Testament, by issuing the first scientific edition. Since then seventy years of work have led to some certain results which are generally accepted.

In the first place no intelligent person who has studied modern criticism holds the old view that each of the four biographies of Jesus is an independent work and an independent testimony to the facts which are related. It is acknowledged that those portions which are common to more than one and are written in identical language have the same origin and represent only one testimony. In the second place, it is allowed that the first Gospel is not the oldest and that the apostle Matthew was not its author. There is also a pretty general agreement that Mark's book is the oldest. The authorship of the fourth Gospel, which like the first was supposed to have been written by an eye-witness, is still contested, but even those who adhere to the tradition admit that it represents a theory about Jesus which is widely different from the view of the three other biographers.

The result is that it can no longer be said that for the life of Jesus there is the evidence of eye-witnesses. The oldest account (Mark) was composed at the earliest some thirty years after the Crucifixion. If such evidence is considered good enough to establish the supernatural events described in that document, there are few alleged supernatural occurrences which we shall not be equally entitled to believe. As a matter of fact, an interval of thirty years makes little difference, for we know that legends require little time to grow. In the East, you will hear of miracles which happened the day before yesterday. The birth of religions is always enveloped in legend, and the miraculous thing would be, as Salomon Reinach has observed, if the story of the birth of Christianity were pure history.

Another disturbing result of unprejudiced examination of the first three Gospels is that, if you take the recorded words of Jesus to be genuine tradition, he had no idea of founding a new religion. And he was fully persuaded that the end of the world was at hand. At present, the chief problem of advanced criticism seems to be whether his entire teaching was not determined by this delusive conviction.

It may be said that the advance of knowledge has thrown no light on one of the most important beliefs that we are asked to accept on authority, the doctrine of immortality. Physiology and psychology have indeed emphasized the difficulties of conceiving a thinking mind without a nervous system. Some are sanguine enough to think that, by scientific examination of psychical phenomena, we may possibly come to know whether the 'spirits' of dead people exist. If the existence of such a world of spirits were ever established, it would possibly be the greatest blow ever sustained by Christianity. For the great appeal of this and of some other religions lies in the promise of a future life of which otherwise we should have no knowledge. If existence after death were proved and became a scientific fact like the law of gravitation, a revealed religion might lose its power. For the whole point of a revealed religion is that it is not based on scientific facts. So far as I know, those who are convinced, by spiritualistic experiments, that they have actual converse with spirits of the dead, and for whom this converse, however delusive the evidence may be, is a fact proved by experience, cease to feel any interest in religion. They possess knowledge and can dispense with faith.

The havoc which science and historical criticism have wrought among orthodox beliefs during the last hundred years was not tamely submitted to, and controversy was not the only weapon employed. Strauss was deprived of his professorship at Tübingen, and his career was ruined. Renan, whose sensational *Life of Jesus* also rejected the supernatural, lost his chair in the Collège de France. Büchner was driven from Tübingen (1855) for his book on *Force and Matter*, which, appealing to the general public, set forth the futility of supernatural explanations of the universe. An attempt was made to chase Haeckel from Jena. In recent years, a French Catholic, the Abbé Loisy, has made notable contributions to the study of the

New Testament and he was rewarded by major excommunication in 1907.

Loisy is the most prominent figure in a growing
movement within the Catholic Church known as
Modernism—a movement which some think is the
gravest crisis in the history of the Church since the
thirteenth century. The Modernists do not form an
organized party; they have no programme. They are
devoted to the Church, to its traditions and associations,
but they look on Christianity as a religion which has
developed, and whose vitality depends upon its continuing to develop. They are bent on reinterpreting
the dogmas in the light of modern science and criticism. The idea of development had already been applied
by Cardinal Newman to Catholic theology. He taught
that it was a natural, and therefore legitimate, development of the primitive creed. But he did not draw the
conclusion which the Modernists draw that if Catholicism is not to lose its power of growth and die, it
must assimilate some of the results of modern thought.
This is what they are attempting to do for it.

Pope Pius x has made every effort to suppress the
Modernists. In 1907 (July) he issued a decree denouncing various results of modern Biblical criticism which
are defended in Loisy's works. The two fundamental
propositions that 'the organic constitution of the
Church is not immutable, but that Christian society
is subject, like every human society, to a perpetual
evolution', and that 'the dogmas which the Church
regards as revealed are not fallen from heaven but are
an interpretation of religious facts at which the human

mind laboriously arrived'—both of which might be deduced from Newman's writings—are condemned. Three months later the Pope issued a long Encyclical letter, containing an elaborate study of Modernist opinions, and ordaining various measures for stamping out the evil. No Modernist would admit that this document represents his views fairly. Yet some of the remarks seem very much to the point. Take one of their books: 'one page might be signed by a Catholic; turn over and you think you are reading the work of a rationalist. In writing history, they make no mention of Christ's divinity; in the pulpit, they proclaim it loudly.'

A plain man may be puzzled by these attempts to retain the letter of old dogmas emptied of their old meaning, and may think it natural enough that the head of the Catholic Church should take a clear and definite stand against the new learning which seems fatal to its fundamental doctrines. For many years past, liberal divines in the Protestant Churches have been doing what the Modernists are doing. The phrase 'Divinity of Christ' is used, but is interpreted so as not to imply a miraculous birth. The Resurrection is preached, but is interpreted so as not to imply a miraculous bodily resurrection. The Bible is said to be an inspired book, but inspiration is used in a vague sense, much as when one says that Plato was inspired; and the vagueness of this new idea of inspiration is even put forward as a merit. Between the extreme views which discard the miraculous altogether, and the old orthodoxy, there are many gradations of belief.

In the Church of England to-day it would be difficult
to say what is the minimum belief required either
from its members or from its clergy. Probably
every leading ecclesiastic would give a different
answer.

The rise of rationalism within the English Church
is interesting and illustrates the relations between
Church and State.

The pietistic movement known as Evangelicalism,
which Wilberforce's *Practical View of Christianity*
(1797) did much to make popular, introduced the
spirit of Methodism within the Anglican Church, and
soon put an end to the delightful type of eighteenth-
century divine, who, as Gibbon says, 'subscribed with
a sigh or a smile' the articles of faith. The rigorous
taboo of the Sabbath was revived, the theatre was
denounced, the corruption of human nature became
the dominant theme, and the Bible more a fetish than
ever. The success of this religious 'reaction', as it is
called, was aided, though not caused, by the common
belief that the French Revolution had been mainly
due to infidelity; the Revolution was taken for an
object lesson showing the value of religion for keeping
the people in order. There was also a religious 'reaction' in France itself. But in both cases this means
not that free thought was less prevalent, but that the
beliefs of the majority were more aggressive and had
powerful spokesmen, while the eighteenth-century
form of rationalism fell out of fashion. A new form of
rationalism, which sought to interpret orthodoxy in
such a liberal way as to reconcile it with philosophy,

was represented by Coleridge who was influenced by German philosophers. Coleridge was a supporter of the Church, and he contributed to the foundation of a school of liberal theology which was to make itself felt after the middle of the century. Newman, the most eminent of the new High Church party, said that he indulged in a liberty of speculation which no Christian could tolerate. The High Church movement which marked the second quarter of the century was as hostile as Evangelicalism to the freedom of religious thought.

The change came after the middle of the century, when the effects of the philosophies of Hegel and Comte, and of foreign Biblical criticism, began to make themselves felt within the English Church. Two remarkable freethinking books appeared at this period which were widely read, F. W. Newman's *Phases of Faith* and W. R. Greg's *Creed of Christendom* (both in 1850). Newman (brother of Cardinal Newman) entirely broke with Christianity, and in his book he describes the mental process by which he came to abandon the beliefs he had once held. Perhaps the most interesting point he makes is the deficiency of the New Testament teaching as a system of morals. Greg was a unitarian. He rejected dogma and inspiration, but he regarded himself as a Christian. Sir J. F. Stephen wittily described his position as that of a disciple 'who had heard the Sermon on the Mount, whose attention had not been called to the Miracles, and who died before the Resurrection'.

There were a few English clergymen (chiefly Oxford

men) who were interested in German criticism and leaned to broad views, which to the Evangelicals and High Churchmen seemed indistinguishable from infidelity. We may call them the Broad Church—though the name did not come in till later. In 1855 Jowett (afterwards Master of Balliol) published an edition of some of St. Paul's Epistles, in which he showed the cloven hoof. It contained an annihilating criticism of the doctrine of the Atonement, an explicit rejection of original sin, and a rationalistic discussion of the question of God's existence. But this and some other unorthodox works of liberal theologians attracted little public attention, though their authors had to endure petty persecution. Five years later, Jowett and some other members of the small liberal group decided to defy the 'abominable system of terrorism which prevents the statement of the plainest fact', and issued a volume of *Essays and Reviews* (1860) by seven writers of whom six were clergymen. The views advocated in these essays seem mild enough to-day, and many of them would be accepted by most well-educated clergymen, but at the time they produced a very painful impression. The authors were called the 'Seven against Christ'. It was laid down that the Bible is to be interpreted like any other book. 'It is not a useful lesson for the young student to apply to Scripture principles which he would hesitate to apply to other books; to make formal reconcilements of discrepancies which he would not think of reconciling in ordinary history; to divide simple words into double meanings; to adopt the fancies or conjectures of Fathers and Commentators as real knowledge.' It is suggested that the Hebrew prophecies do not contain the element of prediction. Contradictory accounts, or accounts which can only be reconciled by conjecture, cannot possibly have been dictated by God. The discrepancies between the genealogies of Jesus in Matthew and Luke, or between the accounts of the Resurrection can be attributed 'neither to any defect in our capacities nor to any reasonable presumption of a hidden wise design, nor to any partial spiritual endowments in the narrators'. The orthodox arguments which lay stress on the assertion of witnesses as the supreme evidence of fact, in support of miraculous occurrences, are set aside on the ground that testimony is a blind guide and can avail nothing against reason and the strong grounds we have for believing in permanent order. It is argued that, under the Thirty-nine Articles, it is permissible to accept as 'parable or poetry or legend' such stories as that of an ass speaking with a man's voice, of waters standing in a solid heap, of witches and a variety of apparitions, and to judge for ourselves of such questions as the personality of Satan or the primeval institution of the Sabbath. The whole spirit of this volume is perhaps expressed in the observation that if any one perceives 'to how great an extent the origin itself of Christianity rests upon *probable* evidence, his principle will relieve him from many difficulties which might otherwise be very disturbing. For relations which may repose on doubtful grounds as matters of history, and, as history, be incapable of being ascertained or verified, may yet be equally suggestive of true ideas with facts absolutely certain'—that is, they may have a spiritual significance although they are historically false.

The most daring Essay was the Rev. Baden Powell's *Study of the Evidences of Christianity*. He was a believer in evolution, who accepted Darwinism, and considered miracles impossible. The volume was denounced by the bishops, and in 1862 two of the contributors, who were beneficed clergymen and thus open to a legal attack, were prosecuted and tried in the Ecclesiastical Court. Condemned on certain points, acquitted on others, they were sentenced to be suspended for a year, and they appealed to the Privy Council. Lord Westbury (Lord Chancellor) pronounced the judgement of the Judicial Committee of the Council, which reversed the decision of the Ecclesiastical Court. The Committee held, among other things, that it is not essential for a clergyman to believe in eternal punishment. This prompted the following epitaph on Lord Westbury: 'Towards the close of his earthly career he dismissed Hell with costs and took away from Orthodox members of the Church of England their last hope of everlasting damnation.'

This was a great triumph for the Broad Church party, and it is an interesting event in the history of the English State-Church. Laymen decided (overruling the opinion of the Archbishops of Canterbury and York) what theological doctrines are and are not binding on a clergyman, and granted within the Church a liberty of opinion which the majority of the Church's representatives regarded as pernicious. This liberty was formally established in 1865 by an Act of Parliament, which altered the form in which clergymen were required to subscribe the Thirty-nine Articles. The episode of *Essays and Reviews* is a landmark in the history of religious thought in England.

The liberal views of the Broad Churchmen and their attitude to the Bible gradually produced some effect upon those who differed most from them; and nowadays there is probably no one who would not admit, at least, that such a passage as Genesis, Chapter XIX might have been composed without the direct inspiration of the Deity.

During the next few years orthodox public opinion was shocked or disturbed by the appearance of several remarkable books which criticized, ignored, or defied authority—Lyell's *Antiquity of Man*, Seeley's *Ecce Homo* (which the pious Lord Shaftesbury said was 'vomited from the jaws of hell'), Lecky's *History of Rationalism*. And a new poet of liberty arose who did not fear to sound the loudest notes of defiance against all that authority held sacred. All the great poets of the nineteenth century were more or less unorthodox; Wordsworth in the years of his highest inspiration was a pantheist; and the greatest of all, Shelley, was a declared atheist. In fearless utterance, in unfaltering zeal against the tyranny of gods and governments, Swinburne was like Shelley. His drama *Atalanta in Calydon* (1865), even though a poet is strictly not answerable for what the persons in his drama say, yet with its denunciation of 'the supreme evil, God,' heralded the coming of a new champion who would defy the fortresses of authority. And in the following year his *Poems and Ballads* expressed the spirit of a pagan who flouted all the prejudices and sanctities of the Christian world.

But the most intense and exciting period of literary warfare against orthodoxy in England began about 1869, and lasted for about a dozen years, during which enemies of dogma, of all complexions, were less reticent and more aggressive than at any other time in the century. Lord Morley has observed that 'the force of speculative literature always hangs on practical opportuneness', and this remark is illustrated by the rationalistic literature of the seventies. It was a time of hope and fear, of progress and danger. Secularists and rationalists were encouraged by the Disestablishment of the Church in Ireland (1869), by the Act which allowed atheists to give evidence in a court of justice (1869), by the abolition of religious tests at all the universities (a measure frequently attempted in vain) in 1871. On the other hand, the Education Act of 1870, progressive though it was, disappointed the advocates of secular education, and was an unwelcome sign of the strength of ecclesiastical influence. Then there was the general alarm felt in Europe by all outside the Roman Church, and by some within it, at the decree of the infallibility of the Pope (by the Vatican Council 1869–70), and an Englishman (Cardinal Manning) was one of the most active spirits in bringing about this decree. It would perhaps have caused less alarm if the Pope's denunciation of modern errors had not been fresh in men's memories. At the end of 1864 he startled the world by issuing a Syllabus 'embracing the principal errors of our age'. Among these were the propositions, that every man is free to adopt and profess the religion he considers true, according to the light of reason; that the Church has no right to employ force; that metaphysics can and ought to be pursued without reference to divine and ecclesiastical authority; that Catholic states are right to allow foreign immigrants to exercise their own religion in public; that the Pope ought to make terms with progress, liberalism, and modern civilization. The document was taken as a declaration of war against enlightenment, and the Vatican Council as the first strategic move of the hosts of darkness. It seemed that the powers of obscurantism were lifting up their heads with a new menace, and there was an instinctive feeling that all the forces of reason should be brought into the field. The history of the last forty years shows that the theory of Infallibility, since it has become a dogma, is not more harmful than it was before. But the efforts of the Catholic Church in the years following the Council to overthrow the French Republic and to rupture the new German Empire were sufficiently disquieting. Against this was to be set the destruction of the temporal power of the Popes and the complete freedom of Italy. This event was the sunrise of Swinburne's *Songs before Sunrise* (which appeared in 1871), a seed-plot of atheism and revolution, sown with implacable hatred of creeds and tyrants. The most wonderful poem in the volume, the *Hymn of Man*, was written while the Vatican Council was sitting. It is a song of triumph over the God of the priests, stricken by the doom of the Pope's temporal power. The concluding verses will show the spirit.

> By thy name that in hellfire was written, and burned
>   at the point of thy sword,
> Thou art smitten, thou God, thou art smitten; thy
>   death is upon thee, O Lord.
> And the lovesong of earth as thou diest resounds
>   through the wind of her wings—
> Glory to Man in the highest! for Man is the master
>   of things.

The fact that such a volume could appear with impunity vividly illustrates the English policy of enforcing the laws for blasphemy only in the case of publications addressed to the masses.

Political circumstances thus invited and stimulated rationalists to come forward boldly, but we must not leave out of account the influence of the Broad Church movement and of Darwinism. The *Descent of Man* appeared precisely in 1871. A new, undogmatic Christianity was being preached in pulpits. Leslie Stephen remarked (1873) that 'it may be said, with little exaggeration, that there is not only no article in the creeds which may not be contradicted with impunity, but that there is none which may not be contradicted in a sermon calculated to win the reputation of orthodoxy and be regarded as a judicious bid for a bishopric. The popular state of mind seems to be typified in the well-known anecdote of the cautious churchwarden, who, whilst commending the general tendency of his incumbent's sermon, felt bound to hazard a protest upon one point. "You see, sir," as he apologetically explained, "I think there be a God." He thought it an error of taste or perhaps of judgement, to hint a doubt as to the first article of the creed.'

The influence exerted among the cultivated classes by the aesthetic movement (Ruskin, Morris, the Pre-Raphaelite painters; then Pater's *Lectures on the Renaissance*, 1873) was also a sign of the times. For the attitude of these critics, artists, and poets was essentially pagan. The saving truths of theology were for them as if they did not exist. The ideal of happiness was found in a region in which heaven was ignored.

The time then seemed opportune for speaking out. Of the unorthodox books and essays,[1] which influenced the young and alarmed believers, in these exciting years, most were the works of men who may be most fairly described by the comprehensive term *agnostics* —a name which had been recently invented by Huxley.

The agnostic holds that there are limits to human reason, and that theology lies outside those limits. Within those limits lies the world with which science (including psychology) deals. Science deals entirely with phenomena, and has nothing to say to the nature of the ultimate reality which may lie behind phenomena. There are four possible attitudes to this ultimate

[1]Besides the works referred to in the text, may be mentioned: Winwood Reade, *Martyrdom of Man*, 1871; Mill, *Three Essays on Religion*; W. R. Cassels, *Supernatural Religion*; Tyndall, *Address to British Association at Belfast*; Huxley, *Animal Automatism*; W. K. Clifford, *Body and Mind*; all in 1874.

reality. There is the attitude of the metaphysician and theologian who are convinced not only that it exists but that it can be at least partly known. There is the attitude of the man who denies that it exists; but he must be also a metaphysician, for its existence can only be disproved by metaphysical arguments. Then there are those who assert that it exists but deny that we can know anything about it. And finally there are those who say that we cannot know whether it exists or not. These last are 'agnostics' in the strict sense of the term, men who *profess not to know*. The third class go beyond phenomena in so far as they assert that there is an ultimate though unknowable reality beneath phenomena. But agnostic is commonly used in a wide sense so as to include the third as well as the fourth class—those who assume an unknowable, as well as those who do not know whether there is an unknowable or not. Comte and Spencer, for instance, who believed in an unknowable, are counted as agnostics. The difference between an agnostic and an atheist is that the atheist positively denies the existence of a personal God, the agnostic does not believe in it.

The writer of this period who held agnosticism in its purest form, and who turned the dry light of reason on to theological opinions with the most merciless logic, was Leslie Stephen. His best-known essay, 'An Agnostic's Apology' (*Fortnightly Review*, 1876), reises the question, have the dogmas of orthodox theologians any meaning? Do they offer, for this is what we want, an intelligible reconciliation of the discords in the universe? It is shown in detail that the various theological explanations of the dealings of God with man, when logically pressed, issue in a confession of ignorance. And what is this but agnosticism? You may call your doubt a mystery, but mystery is only the theological phrase for agnosticism. 'Why, when no honest man will deny in private that every ultimate problem is wrapped in the profoundest mystery, do honest men proclaim in pulpits that unhesitating certainty is the duty of the most foolish and ignorant? We are a company of ignorant beings, dimly discerning light enough for our daily needs, but hopelessly differing whenever we attempt to describe the ultimate origin or end of our paths; and yet, when one of us ventures to declare that we don't know the map of the Universe as well as the map of our infinitesimal parish, he is hooted, reviled and perhaps told that he will be damned to all eternity for his faithlessness.' The characteristic of Leslie Stephen's essays is that they are less directed to showing that orthodox theology is untrue as that there is no reality about it, and that its solutions of difficulties are sham solutions. If it solved any part of the mystery, it would be welcome, but it does not, it only adds new difficulties. It is 'a mere edifice of moonshine'. The writer makes no attempt to prove by logic that ultimate reality lies outside the limits of human reason. He bases this conclusion on the fact that all philosophers hopelessly contradict one another; if the subject-matter of philosophy were, like physical science, within the reach of the intelligence, some agreement must have been reached.

The Broad Church movement, the attempts to liberalize Christianity, to pour its old wine into new bottles, to make it unsectarian and undogmatic, to find compromises between theology and science, found no favour in Leslie Stephen's eyes, and he criticized all this with a certain contempt. There was a controversy about the efficacy of prayer. Is it reasonable, for instance, to pray for rain? Here science and theology were at issue on a practical point which comes within the domain of science. Some theologians adopted the compromise that to pray against an eclipse would be foolish, but to pray for rain might be sensible. 'One phenomenon', Stephen wrote, 'is just as much the result of fixed causes as the other; but it is easier for the imagination to suppose the interference of a divine agent to be hidden away somewhere amidst the infinitely complex play of forces, which elude our calculations in meteorological phenomena, than to believe in it where the forces are simple enough to admit of prediction. The distinction is of course invalid in a scientific sense. Almighty power can interfere as easily with the events which are, as with those which are not, in the Nautical Almanac. One cannot suppose that God retreats as science advances, and that he spoke in thunder and lightning till Franklin unravelled the laws of their phenomena.'

Again, when a controversy about hell engaged public attention, and some otherwise orthodox theologians bethought themselves that eternal punishment was a horrible doctrine and then found that the evidence for it was not quite conclusive and were bold enough to say so, Leslie Stephen stepped in to point out that, if so, historical Christianity deserves all that its most virulent enemies have said about it in this respect. When the Christian creed really ruled men's consciences, nobody could utter a word against the truth of the dogma of hell. If that dogma had not an intimate organic connection with the creed, if it had been a mere unimportant accident, it could not have been so vigorous and persistent wherever Christianity was strongest. The attempt to eliminate it or soften it down is a sign of decline. 'Now, at last, your creed is decaying. People have discovered that you know nothing about it; that heaven and hell belong to dreamland; that the impertinent young curate who tells me that I shall be burnt everlastingly for not sharing his superstition is just as ignorant as I am myself, and that I know as much as my dog. And then you calmly say again, "It is all a mistake. Only believe in a something—and we will make it as easy for you as possible. Hell shall have no more than a fine equable temperature, really good for the constitution; there shall be nobody in it except Judas Iscariot and one or two others; and even the poor Devil shall have a chance if he will resolve to mend his ways." '

Matthew Arnold may, I suppose, be numbered among the agnostics, but he was of a very different type. He introduced a new kind of criticism of the Bible—literary criticism. Deeply concerned for morality and religion, a supporter of the Established Church, he took the Bible under his special protection, and in three works, *St. Paul and Protestantism* (1870),

Literature and Dogma (1873), and *God and the Bible* (1875), he endeavoured to rescue that book from its orthodox exponents, whom he regarded as the corrupters of Christianity. It would be just, he says, 'but hardly perhaps Christian' to fling back the word infidel at the orthodox theologians for their bad literary and scientific criticisms of the Bible and to speak of 'the torrent of infidelity which pours every Sunday from our pulpits!' The corruption of Christianity has been due to theology 'with its insane licence of affirmation about God, its insane licence of affirmation about immortality'; to the hypothesis of 'a magnified and non-natural man at the head of mankind's and the world's affairs'; and the fancy account of God 'made up by putting scattered expressions of the Bible together and taking them literally'. He chastises with urbane persiflage the knowledge which the orthodox think they possess about the proceedings and plans of God. 'To think they know what passed in the Council of the Trinity is not hard to them; they could easily think they even knew what were the hangings of the Trinity's council-chamber.' Yet 'the very expression, *the Trinity*, jars with the whole idea and character of Bible-religion; but, lest the Socinian should be unduly elated at hearing this, let us hasten to add that so too, and just as much, does the expression, a great Personal First Cause'. He uses *God* as the least inadequate name for that universal order which the intellect feels after as a law, and the heart feels after as a benefit; and defines it as 'the stream of tendency by which all things strive to fulfil the law of their being'. He

defined it further as a Power that makes for righteousness, and thus went considerably beyond the agnostic
position. He was impatient of the minute criticism
which analyses the Biblical documents and discovers
inconsistencies and absurdities, and he did not appreciate the importance of the comparative study of
religions. But when we read of a dignitary in a recent
Church congress laying down that the narratives in
the books of Jonah and Daniel must be accepted
because Jesus quoted them, we may wish that Arnold
were here to reproach the orthodox for 'want of
intellectual seriousness'.

These years also saw the appearance of John Morley's
sympathetic studies of the French freethinkers of the
eighteenth century, *Voltaire* (1872), *Rousseau* (1873),
and *Diderot* (1878). He edited the *Fortnightly Review*,
and for some years this journal was distinguished by
brilliant criticisms on the popular religion, contributed
by able men writing from many points of view. A
part of the book which he afterwards published under
the title *Compromise* appeared in the *Fortnightly* in
1874. In *Compromise* 'the whole system of objective
propositions which make up the popular belief of the
day' is condemned as mischievous, and it is urged
that those who disbelieve should speak out plainly.
Speaking out is an intellectual duty. Englishmen have
a strong sense of political responsibility, and a corres-
pondingly weak sense of intellectual responsibility.
Even minds that are not commonplace are affected
for the worse by the political spirit which 'is the great
force in throwing love of truth and accurate reasoning

into a secondary place'. And the principles which have prevailed in politics have been adopted by theology for her own use. In the one case, convenience first, truth second; in the other, emotional comfort first, truth second. If the immorality is less gross in the case of religion, there is 'the stain of intellectual improbity'. And this is a crime against society, for 'they who tamper with veracity from whatever motive are tampering with the vital force of human progress'. The intellectual insincerity which is here blamed is just as prevalent to-day. The English have not changed their nature, the 'political' spirit is still rampant, and we are ruled by the view that because compromise is necessary in politics it is also a good thing in the intellectual domain.

The *Fortnightly* under Morley's guidance was an effective organ of enlightenment. I have no space to touch on the works of other men of letters and of men of science in these combative years, but it is to be noted that, while denunciations of modern thought poured from the pulpits, a popular diffusion of freethought was carried on, especially by Bradlaugh in public lectures and in his paper, the *National Reformer*, not without collisions with the civil authorities.

If we take the cases in which the civil authorities in England have intervened to repress the publication of unorthodox opinions during the last two centuries, we find that the object has always been to prevent the spread of freethought among the masses. The victims have been either poor, uneducated people, or men who propagated free thought in a popular form. I touched upon this before in speaking of Paine, and it is borne out by the prosecutions of the nineteenth and twentieth centuries. The unconfessed motive has been fear of the people. Theology has been regarded as a good instrument for keeping the poor in order, and unbelief as a cause of accompaniment of dangerous political opinions. The idea has not altogether disappeared that free thought is peculiarly indecent in the poor, that it is highly desirable to keep them superstitious in order to keep them contented, that they should be duly thankful for all the theological as well as social arrangements which have been made for them by their betters. I may quote from an essay of Frederic Harrison an anecdote which admirably expresses the becoming attitude of the poor towards ecclesiastical institutions. 'The master of a workhouse in Essex was once called in to act as chaplain to a dying pauper. The poor soul faintly murmured some hopes of heaven. But this the master abruptly cut short and warned him to turn his last thoughts towards hell. "And thankful you ought to be", said he, "that you have a hell to go to." '

The most important English freethinkers who appealed to the masses were Holyoake,[1] the apostle of 'secularism', and Bradlaugh. The great achievement for which Bradlaugh will be best remembered was the

[1] It may be noted that Holyoake towards the end of his life helped to found the Rationalist Press Association, of which Edward Clodd was for many years Chairman. This is the chief society in England for propagating rationalism, and its main object is to diffuse in a cheap form the works of freethinkers of mark. I understand [1913] that more than two million copies of its cheap reprints have been sold.

securing of the right of unbelievers to sit in Parliament without taking an oath (1888). The chief work to which Holyoake (who in his early years was imprisoned for blasphemy) contributed was the abolition of taxes on the Press, which seriously hampered the popular diffusion of knowledge.[1] In England, censorship of the Press had long ago disappeared (above, p. 110); in most other European countries it was abolished in the course of the nineteenth century.[2]

In the progressive countries of Europe there has been a marked growth of tolerance (I do not mean legal toleration, but the tolerance of public opinion), during the last thirty years. A generation ago Lord Morley wrote: 'The preliminary stage has scarcely been reached—the stage in which public opinion grants to every one the unrestricted right of shaping his own beliefs, independently of those of the people who surround him.' I think this preliminary stage has now been passed. Take England. We are now far from the days when Arnold would have sent the elder Mill to Botany Bay for irreligious opinions. But we are also far from the days when Darwin's *Descent* created an uproar. Darwin has been buried in Westminster Abbey. To-day books can appear denying the historical existence of Jesus without causing any commotion.

[1] The advertisement tax was abolished in 1853, the stamp tax in 1855, the paper duty in 1861, and the optional duty in 1870.

[2] In Austria-Hungary the police have the power to suppress printed matter provisionally. In Russia the Press was declared free in 1905 by an Imperial decree, which, however, has become a dead letter. The newspapers are completely under the control of the police.

It may be doubted whether what Lord Action wrote in 1877 would be true now: 'There are in our day many educated men who think it right to persecute.' In 1895, Lecky was a candidate for the representation of Dublin University. His rationalistic opinions were indeed brought up against him, but he was successful, though the majority of the constituents were orthodox. In the seventies his candidature would have been hopeless. The old commonplace that a freethinker is sure to be immoral is no longer heard. We may say that we have now reached a stage at which it is admitted by every one who counts (except at the Vatican), that there is nothing in earth or heaven which may not legitimately be treated without any of the assumptions which in old days authority used to impose.

In this brief review of the triumphs of reason in the nineteenth century, we have been considering the discoveries of science and criticism which made the old orthodoxy logically untenable. But the advance in freedom of thought, the marked difference in the general attitude of men in all lands towards theological authority to-day from the attitude of a hundred years ago, cannot altogether be explained by the power of logic. It is not so much criticism of old ideas as the appearance of new ideas and interests that changes the views of men at large. It is not logical demonstrations but new social conceptions that bring about a general transformation of attitude towards ultimate problems. Now the idea of the progress of the human race must, I think, be held largely answerable for this change of attitude. It must, I think, be held to have operated powerfully as a solvent of theological beliefs. I have spoken of the teaching of Diderot and his friends that man's energies should be devoted to making the earth pleasant. A new ideal was substituted for the old ideal based on theological propositions. It inspired the English Utilitarian philosophers (Bentham, James Mill, J. S. Mill, Grote) who preached the greatest happiness of the greatest number as the supreme object of action and the basis of morality. This ideal was powerfully reinforced by the doctrine of historical progress, which was started in France (1750) by Turgot, who made progress the organic principle of history. It was developed by Condorcet (1793), and put forward by Priestley in England. The idea was seized upon by the French socialistic philosophers, Saint-Simon and Fourier. The optimism of Fourier went so far as to anticipate the time when the sea would be turned by man's ingenuity into lemonade, when there would be 37 million poets as great as Homer, 37 million writers as great as Molière, 37 million men of science equal to Newton. But it was Comte who gave the doctrine weight and power. His social philosophy and his religion of Humanity are based upon it. The triumphs of science endorsed it; it has been associated with, though it is not necessarily implied in, the scientific theory of evolution; and it is perhaps fair to say that it has been the guiding spiritual force of the nineteenth century. It has introduced the new ethical principle of duty to posterity. We shall hardly be far wrong if we say that the new interest in the future and the progress of the race has done a great deal to undermine unconsciously the old interest in a life beyond the grave; and it has dissolved the blighting doctrine of the radical corruption of man.

Nowhere has the theory of progress been more emphatically recognized than in the Monistic movement which has been exciting great interest in Germany (1910–12). This movement is based on the ideas of Haeckel, who is looked up to as the master, but those ideas have been considerably changed under the influence of Ostwald, the new leader. While Haeckel is a biologist, Ostwald's brilliant work was done in chemistry and physics. The new Monism differs from the old, in the first place, in being much less dogmatic. It declares that all that is in our experience can be the object of a corresponding science. It is much more a method than a system, for its sole ultimate object is to comprehend all human experience in unified knowledge. Secondly, while it maintains, with Haeckel, evolution as the guiding principle in the history of living things, it rejects his pantheism and his theory of thinking atoms. The old mechanical theory of the physical world has been gradually supplanted by the theory of energy, and Ostwald, who was one of the foremost exponents of energy, has made it a leading idea of Monism. What has been called matter is, so far as we know now, simply a complex of energies, and he has sought to extend the 'energetic' principle from physical or chemical to biological, psychical, and social phenomena. But it is to be observed that no finality is claimed for the conception of energy; it is simply an hypothesis which corresponds to our present stage of knowledge, and may, as knowledge advances, be superseded.

Monism resembles the positive philosophy and religion of Comte in so far as it means an outlook on life based entirely on science and excluding theology, mysticism, and metaphysics. It may be called a religion, if we adopt MacTaggart's definition of religion as 'an emotion resting on a conviction of the harmony between ourselves and the universe at large'. But it is much better not to use the word religion in connexion with it, and the Monists have no thought of founding a Monistic, as Comte founded a Positivist, church. They insist upon the sharp opposition between the outlook of science and the outlook of religion, and find the mark of spiritual progress in the fact that religion is gradually becoming less indispensable. The further we go back in the past, the more valuable is religion as an element in civilization; as we advance, it retreats more and more into the background, to be replaced by science. Religions have been, in principle, pessimistic, so far as the present world is concerned; Monism is, in principle, optimistic, for it recognizes that the process of his evolution has overcome, in increasing measure, the bad element in man, and will go on overcoming it still more. Monism proclaims that development and progress are the practical principles of human conduct, while the Churches, especially the Catholic Church, have been steadily conservative, and though they have been unable to put a stop to progress have endeavoured to suppress its symptoms—to bottle up the steam.[1] The Monistic congress at Hamburg in 1911 had a success which surprised its promoters. The movement bids fair to be a powerful influence in diffusing rationalistic thought.[2]

If we take the three large States of Western Europe, in which the majority of Christians are Catholics, we see how the ideal of progress, freedom of thought, and the decline of ecclesiastical power go together. In Spain, where the Church has enormous power and wealth and can still dictate to the Court and the politicians, the idea of progress, which is vital in France and Italy, has not yet made its influence seriously felt. Liberal thought indeed is widely spread in the small educated class, but the great majority of the whole population are illiterate, and it is the interest of the Church to keep them so. The education of the people, as all enlightened Spaniards confess, is the pressing need of the country. How formidable are the obstacles which will have to be overcome before modern education is allowed to spread was shown by the tragedy of Francisco Ferrer, which reminded everybody that in one corner of Western Europe the mediaeval spirit is still vigorous. Ferrer had devoted himself to the founding of modern schools in the

[1] I have taken these points, illustrating the Monistic attitude to the Churches, from Ostwald's *Monistic Sunday Sermons* (German), 1911, 1912.

[2] I may note here that, as this is not a history of thought, I make no reference to recent philosophical speculations (in America, England, and France) which are sometimes claimed as tending to bolster up theology. But they are all profoundly unorthodox.

province of Catalonia (since 1901). He was a rationalist, and his schools, which had a marked success, were entirely secular. The ecclesiastical authorities execrated him, and in the summer of 1909 chance gave them the means of destroying him. A strike of workmen at Barcelona developed into a violent revolution, Ferrer happened to be in Barcelona for some days at the beginning of the movement, with which he had no connection whatever, and his enemies seized the opportunity to make him responsible for it. False evidence (including forged documents) was manufactured. Evidence which would have helped his case was suppressed. The Catholic papers agitated against him, and the leading ecclesiastics of Barcelona urged the government not to spare the man who founded the modern schools, the root of all the trouble. Ferrer was condemned by a military tribunal and shot (13th Oct.). He suffered in the cause of reason and freedom of thought, though, as there is no longer an Inquisition, his enemies had to kill him under the false charge of anarchy and treason. It is possible that the indignation which was felt in Europe and was most loudly expressed in France may prevent the repetition of such extreme measures, but almost anything may happen in a country where the Church is so powerful and so bigoted, and the politicians so corrupt.

Chapter VIII

THE JUSTIFICATION OF LIBERTY OF THOUGHT

MOST men who have been brought up in the free atmosphere of a modern State sympathize with liberty in its long struggle with authority and may find it difficult to see that anything can be said for the tyrannical, and as they think extraordinarily perverse, policy by which communities and governments persistently sought to stifle new ideas and suppress free speculation. The conflict sketched in these pages appears as a war between light and darkness. We exclaim that altar and throne formed a sinister conspiracy against the progress of humanity. We look back with horror at the things which so many champions of reason endured at the hands of blind, if not malignant, bearers of authority.

But a more or less plausible case can be made out for coercion. Let us take the most limited view of the lawful powers of society over its individual members. Let us lay down, with Mill, that 'the sole end for which mankind are warranted, individually and collectively, in interfering with the liberty of action of any of their members is self-protection', and that coercion is only justified for the prevention of harm to others. This is the minimum claim the State can make, and it will be admitted that it is not only the right but the duty of the State to prevent harm to its members. That is what it is for. Now no abstract or independent principle is discoverable, why liberty of speech should be a privileged form of liberty of action, or why society should lay down its arms of defence and fold its hands, when it is persuaded that harm is threatened to it through the speech of any of its members. The government has to judge of the danger, and its judgement may be wrong; but if it is convinced that harm is being done, is it not its plain duty to interfere?

This argument supplies an apology for the suppression of free opinion by governments in ancient and modern times. It can be urged for the Inquisition, for censorship of the press, for blasphemy laws, for all coercive measures of the kind, that, if excessive or ill-judged, they were intended to protect society against what their authors sincerely believed to be grave injury, and were simple acts of duty. (This apology, of course, does not extend to acts done for the sake of the alleged good of the victims themselves, namely, to secure their future salvation.)

Nowadays we condemn all such measures and disallow the right of the State to interfere with the free expression of opinion. So deeply is the doctrine of liberty seated in our minds that we find it difficult to make allowances for the coercive practices of our misguided ancestors. How is this doctrine justified? It rests on no abstract basis, on no principle independent of society itself, but entirely on considerations of utility.

We saw how Socrates indicated the social value of freedom of discussion. We saw how Milton observed that such freedom was necessary for the advance of knowledge. But in the period during which the cause of toleration was fought for and practically won, the argument more generally used was the injustice of punishing a man for opinions which he honestly held and could not help holding, since conviction is not a matter of will; in other words, the argument that error is not a crime and that it is therefore unjust to punish it. This argument, however, does not prove the case for freedom of discussion. The advocate of coercion may reply: We admit that it is unjust to punish a man for private erroneous beliefs; but it is not unjust to forbid the propagation of such beliefs if we are convinced that they are harmful; it is not unjust to punish him, not for holding them, but for publishing them. The truth is that, in examining principles, the word *just* is misleading. All the virtues are based on experience, physiological or social, and justice is no exception. *Just* designates a class of rules or principles of which the social utility has been found by experience to be paramount and which are recognized to be so important as to override all considerations of immediate expediency. And social utility is the only test. It is futile, therefore, to say to a government that it acts unjustly in coercing opinion, unless it is shown that freedom of opinion is a principle of such overmastering social utility as to render other considerations negligible. Socrates had a true instinct in taking the line that freedom is valuable to society.

The reasoned justification of liberty of thought is due to J. S. Mill, who set it forth in his work *On*

Liberty, published in 1859. This book treats of liberty in general, and attempts to fix the frontier of the region in which individual freedom should be considered absolute and unassailable. The second chapter considers liberty of thought and discussion, and if many may think that Mill unduly minimized the functions of society, underrating its claims as against the individual, few will deny the justice of the chief arguments or question the general soundness of his conclusions.

Pointing out that no fixed standard was recognized for testing the propriety of the interference on the part of the community with its individual members, he finds the test in self-protection, that is, the prevention of harm to others. He bases the principle not on abstract rights, but on 'utility, in the largest sense, grounded on the permanent interests of man as a progressive being'. He then uses the following argument to show that to silence opinion and discussion is always contrary to those permanent interests. Those who would suppress an opinion (it is assumed that they are honest) deny its truth, but they are not infallible. They may be wrong, or right, or partly wrong and partly right. (1) If they are wrong and the opinion they would crush is true, they have robbed, or done their utmost to rob, mankind of a truth. They will say: But we were justified, for we exercised our judgement to the best of our ability, and are we to be told that because our judgement is fallible we are not to use it? We forbade the propagation of an opinion which we were sure was false and pernicious; this implies no greater claim to infallibility than any act done by public authority. If we are to act at all, we must assume our own opinion to be true. To this Mill acutely replies: 'There is the greatest difference between assuming an opinion to be true, because with every opportunity for contesting it it has not been refuted, and assuming its truth for the purpose of not permitting its refutation. Complete liberty of contradicting and disproving our opinion is the very condition which justifies us in assuming its truth for purposes of action, and on no other terms can a being with human faculties have any rational assurance of being right.'

(2) If the received opinion which it is sought to protect against the intrusion of error, is true, the suppression of discussion is still contrary to general utility. A received opinion may happen to be true (it is very seldom entirely true); but a rational certainty that it is so can only be secured by the fact that it has been fully canvassed but has not been shaken.

Commoner and more important is (3) the case where the conflicting doctrines share the truth between them. Here Mill has little difficulty in proving the utility of supplementing one-sided popular truths by other truths which popular opinion omits to consider. And he observes that if either of the opinions which share the truth has a claim not merely to be tolerated but to be encouraged, it is the one which happens to be held by the minority, since this is the one 'which for the time being represents the neglected interests'. He takes the doctrines of Rousseau, which might conceivably have been suppressed as pernicious. To the self-complacent eighteenth century those doctrines came as 'a salutary shock, dislocating the compact mass of one-sided opinion'. The current opinions were indeed nearer to the truth than Rousseau's, they contained much less of error; 'nevertheless there lay in Rousseau's doctrine, and has floated down the stream of opinion along with it, a considerable amount of exactly those truths which the popular opinion wanted; and these are the deposit which was left behind when the flood subsided'.

Such is the drift of Mill's main argument. The present writer would prefer to state the justification of freedom of opinion[1] in a somewhat different form, though in accordance with Mill's reasoning. The progress of civilization, if it is partly conditioned by circumstances beyond man's control, depends more, and in an increasing measure, on things which are within his own power. Prominent among these are the advancement of knowledge and the deliberate adaptation of his habits and institutions to new conditions. To advance knowledge and to correct errors, unrestricted freedom of discussion is required. History shows that knowledge grew when speculation was perfectly free in Greece, and that in modern times, since restrictions on inquiry have been entirely removed, it has advanced with a velocity which would seem diabolical to the slaves of the mediaeval Church. Then, it is obvious that in order to readjust social customs,

[1]This paragraph together with the paragraph on page 195 beginning, 'Once the principle of liberty of thought is accepted', contain the key propositions of Bury's argument. —H.J.B.

institutions, and methods to new needs and circumstances, there must be unlimited freedom of canvassing and criticizing them, of expressing the most unpopular opinions, no matter how offensive to prevailing sentiment they may be. If the history of civilization has any lesson to teach it is this: there is one supreme condition of mental and moral progress which it is completely within the power of man himself to secure, and that is perfect liberty of thought and discussion. The establishment of this liberty may be considered the most valuable achievement of modern civilization, and as a condition of social progress it should be deemed fundamental. The considerations of permanent utility on which it rests must outweigh any calculations of present advantage which from time to time might be thought to demand its violation.

It is evident that this whole argument depends on the assumption that the progress of the race, its intellectual and moral development, is a reality and is valuable. The argument will not appeal to any one who holds with Cardinal Newman that 'our race's progress and perfectibility is a dream, because revelation contradicts it'; and he may consistently subscribe to the same writer's conviction that 'it would be a gain to this country were it vastly more superstitious, more bigoted, more gloomy, more fierce in its religion, than at present it shows itself to be'.

While Mill was writing his brilliant Essay, which every one should read, the English government of the day (1858) instituted prosecutions for the circulation of the doctrine that it is lawful to put tyrants to death, on the ground that the doctrine is immoral. Fortunately the prosecutions were not persisted in. Mill refers to the matter, and maintains that such a doctrine as tyrannicide (and, let us add, anarchy) does not form any exception to the rule that 'there ought to exist the fullest liberty of professing and discussing, as a matter of ethical conviction, any doctrine, however immoral it may be considered'.

Exceptions, cases where the interference of the authorities is proper, are only apparent, for they really come under another rule. For instance, if there is a direct instigation to particular acts of violence, there may be a legitimate case for interference. But the incitement must be deliberate and direct. If I write a book condemning existing societies and defending a theory of anarchy, and a man who reads it presently commits an outrage, it may clearly be established that my book made the man an anarchist and induced him to commit the crime, but it would be illegitimate to punish[1] me or suppress the book unless it contained a direct incitement to the specific crime which he committed.

[1]Writers in France after the war were punished for the consequences of their writings, notably Charles Maurras, who did plead his right to freedom of speech and publication under the law; it was held that since many young men who had been misled by his writings had either suffered or been punished for their actions, it would be unjust that he who was responsible for their fault and their fate should go unpunished. The ordinances under which these proceedings were instituted and the courts in which they were carried out have been impugned as illegal. But a strict legality would have seemed legal injustice to the outraged half of the country. Bury's principle assumes a settled common political order in which ultimate issues are not forced.—H.J.B.

It is conceivable that difficult cases might arise where a government might be strongly tempted, and might be urged by public clamour, to violate the principle of liberty. Let us suppose a case, very improbable, but which will make the issue clear and definite. Imagine that a man of highly magnetic personality, endowed with a wonderful power of infecting others with his own ideas however irrational, in short a typical religious leader, is convinced that the world will come to an end in the course of a few months. He goes about the country preaching and distributing pamphlets; his words have an electrical effect: and the masses of the uneducated and half-educated are persuaded that they have indeed only a few weeks to prepare for the day of judgement. Multitudes leave their occupations, abandon their work, in order to spend the short time that remains in prayer and listening to the exhortations of the prophet. The country is paralysed by the gigantic strike; traffic and industries come to a standstill. The people have a perfect legal right to give up their work, and the prophet has a perfect legal right to propagate his opinion that the end of the world is at hand—an opinion which Jesus Christ and his followers in their day held quite as erroneously. It would be said that desperate ills have desperate remedies, and there would be a strong temptation to suppress the fanatic. But to arrest a man who is not breaking the law or exhorting any one to break it, or causing a breach of the peace, would be an act of glaring tyranny. Many will hold that the evil of setting back the clock of liberty would outbalance all the temporary evils, great as they might be, caused by the propagation of a delusion. It would be absurd to deny that liberty of speech may sometimes cause particular harm. Every good thing sometimes does harm. Government, for instance, which makes fatal mistakes; law, which so often bears hardly and inequitably in individual cases. And can the Christians urge any other plea for their religion when they are unpleasantly reminded that it has caused untold suffering by its principle of exclusive salvation?

Once the principle of liberty of thought is accepted as a supreme condition of social progress, it passes from the sphere of ordinary expediency into the sphere of higher expediency which we call justice. In other words it becomes a right on which every man should be able to count. The fact that this right is ultimately based on utility does not justify a government in curtailing it, on the ground of utility, in particular cases.

The recent rather alarming inflictions of penalties for blasphemy in England illustrate this point. It was commonly supposed that the blasphemy laws (see above, p. 110), though unrepealed, were a dead letter. But since December 1911 half a dozen persons have been imprisoned for this offence. In these cases Christian doctrines were attacked by poor and more or less uneducated persons in language which may be described as coarse and offensive. Some of the judges seem to have taken the line that it is not blasphemy to attack the fundamental doctrines provided 'the decencies of controversy' are preserved, but that 'indecent' attacks constitute blasphemy. This implies a new definition of legal blasphemy, and is entirely contrary to the intention of the laws. Sir J. F. Stephen pointed out that the decisions of judges from the time of Lord Hale (seventeenth century) to the trial of Foote (1883) laid down the same doctrine and based it on the same principle: the doctrine being that it is a crime either to deny the truth of the fundamental doctrines of the Christian religion or to hold them up to contempt or ridicule; and the principle being that Christianity is a part of the law of the land.

The apology offered for such prosecutions is that their object is to protect religious sentiment from insult and ridicule. Sir J. F. Stephen observed: 'If the law were really impartial and punished blasphemy only because it offends the feelings of believers, it ought also to punish such preaching as offends the feelings of unbelievers. All the more earnest and enthusiastic forms of religion are extremely offensive to those who do not believe them.' If the law does not in any sense recognize the truth of Christian doctrine, it would have to apply the same rule to the Salvation Army. In fact the law 'can be explained and justified only on what I regard as its true principle—the principle of persecution'. The opponents of Christianity may justly say: If Christianity is false, why is it to be attacked only in polite language? Its goodness depends on its truth. If you grant its falsehood, you cannot maintain that it deserves special protection. But the law imposes no restraint on the Christian, however offensive his teaching may be to those who do not agree with him;

therefore it is not based on an impartial desire to prevent the use of language which causes offence; therefore it is based on the hypothesis that Christianity is true; and therefore its principle is persecution.

Of course, the present administration of the common law in regard to blasphemy does not endanger the liberty of those unbelievers who have the capacity for contributing to progress. But it violates the supreme principle of liberty of opinion and discussion. It hinders uneducated people from saying in the only ways in which they know how to say it, what those who have been brought up differently say, with impunity, far more effectively and far more insidiously. Some of the men who have been imprisoned during the last two years [1911–13], only uttered in language of deplorable taste views that are expressed more or less politely in books which are in the library of a bishop unless he is a very ignorant person, and against which the law, if it has any validity, ought to have been enforced. Thus the law, as now administered, simply penalizes bad taste and places disabilities upon uneducated freethinkers. If their words offend their audience so far as to cause a disturbance, they should be prosecuted for a breach of public order,[1] not because their words are blasphemous. A man who robs or injures a church, or even an episcopal palace, is not prosecuted for sacrilege but for larceny or malicious damage or something of the kind.

[1]Blasphemy is an offence in Germany; but it must be proved that offence has actually been given, and the penalty does not exceed imprisonment for three days.

The abolition of penalties for blasphemy was proposed in the House of Commons (by Bradlaugh) in 1889 and rejected. The reform is urgently needed. It would 'prevent the recurrence at irregular intervals of scandalous prosecutions which have never in any one instance benefited any one, least of all the cause which they were intended to serve, and which sometimes afford a channel for the gratification of private malice under the cloak of religion'.[1]

The struggle of reason against authority has ended in what appears now to be a decisive and permanent victory for liberty. In the most civilized and progressive countries, freedom of discussion is recognized as a fundamental principle. In fact, we may say it is accepted as a test of enlightenment, and the man in the street is forward in acknowledging that countries like Russia and Spain, where opinion is more or less fettered, must on that account be considered less civilized than their neighbours. All intellectual people who count take it for granted that there is no subject in heaven or earth which ought not to be investigated without any deference or reference to theological assumptions. No man of science has any fear of publishing his researches, whatever consequences they may involve for current beliefs. Criticism of religious doctrines and of political and social institutions is free. Hopeful people may feel confident that the victory is permanent; that intellectual freedom is now assured to mankind as a possession

[1] The quotations are from Sir J. F. Stephen's article, 'Blasphemy and Blasphemous Libel', in the *Fortnightly Review*, March 1884, pp. 289-318.

for ever; that the future will see the collapse of those forces which still work against it and its gradual diffusion in the more backward parts of the earth. Yet history may suggest that this prospect is not assured. Can we be certain that there may not come a great set-back? For freedom of discussion and speculation was, as we saw, fully realized in the Greek and Roman world, and then an unforeseen force, in the shape of Christianity, came in and laid chains upon the human mind and suppressed freedom and imposed upon man a weary struggle to recover the freedom which he had lost. Is it not conceivable that something of the same kind may occur again? that some new force, emerging from the unknown, may surprise the world and cause a similar set-back?

The possibility cannot be denied, but there are some considerations which render it improbable (apart from a catastrophe sweeping away European culture). There are certain radical differences between the intellectual situation now and in antiquity. The facts known to the Greeks about the nature of the physical universe were few. Much that was taught was not proved. Compare what they knew and what we know about astronomy and geography—to take the two branches in which (besides mathematics) they made most progress. When there were so few demonstrated facts to work upon, there was the widest room for speculation. Now to suppress a number of rival theories in favour of one is a very different thing from suppressing whole systems of established facts. If one school of astronomers holds that the earth goes round the sun,

another that the sun goes round the earth, but neither
is able to demonstrate its proposition, it is easy for
an authority, which has coercive power, to suppress
one of them successfully. But once it is agreed by all
astronomers that the earth goes round the sun, it is a
hopeless task for any authority to compel men to
accept a false view. In short, because she is in possession of a vast mass of ascertained facts about the nature
of the universe, reason holds a much stronger position
now than at the time when Christian theology led her
captive. All these facts are her fortifications. Again, it
is difficult to see what can arrest the continuous progress of knowledge in the future. In ancient times this
progress depended on a few; nowadays, many nations
take part in the work. A general conviction of the
importance of science prevails to-day, which did not
prevail in Greece. And the circumstance that the advance of material civilization depends on science is
perhaps a practical guarantee that scientific research
will not come to an abrupt halt. In fact science is now
a social institution, as much as religion.

But if science seems pretty safe, it is always possible
that in countries where the scientific spirit is held in
honour, nevertheless, serious restrictions may be laid
on speculations touching social, political and religious
questions. Russia has men of science inferior to none,
and Russia has its notorious censorship. It is by no
means inconceivable that in lands where opinion is
now free coercion might be introduced. If a revolutionary social movement prevailed, led by men inspired
by faith in formulas (like the men of the French

Revolution) and resolved to impose their creed, experience shows that coercion would almost inevitably be resorted to. Nevertheless, while it would be silly to suppose that attempts may not be made in the future to put back the clock, liberty is in a far more favourable position now than under the Roman Empire. For at that time the social importance of freedom of opinion was not appreciated, whereas now, in consequence of the long conflict which was necessary in order to re-establish it, men consciously realize its value. Perhaps this conviction will be strong enough to resist all conspiracies against liberty. Meanwhile, nothing should be left undone to impress upon the young that freedom of thought is an axiom of human progress. It may be feared, however, that this is not likely to be done for a long time to come. For our methods of early education are founded on authority. It is true that children are sometimes exhorted to think for themselves. But the parent or instructor who gives this excellent advice is confident that the results of the child's thinking for himself will agree with the opinions which his elders consider desirable. It is assumed that he will reason from principles which have already been instilled into him by authority. But if his thinking for himself takes the form of questioning these principles, whether moral or religious, his parents and teachers, unless they are very exceptional persons, will be extremely displeased, and will certainly discourage him. It is, of course, only singularly promising children whose freedom of thought will go so far. In this sense it might be said that 'distrust thy father and

mother' is the first commandment with promise. It
should be a part of education to explain to children,
as soon as they are old enough to understand, when it
is reasonable, and when it is not, to accept what they
are told, on authority.

EPILOGUE
By H. J. Blackham

BURY'S prescient recognition in his concluding pages that attempts might be made to put back the clock throws a thin line across the gulf which the cataclysmic events of these forty years have put between his standpoint and ours. Throughout this time, war has been the social medium in which all things have taken place, for it has either enveloped all in its whirlwind or involved all in the wreckage and dislocation it has left behind or overshadowed all with the fatality of its obvious coming on. Crisis has overhung a generation. In such rough times, the social utility of freedom of thought is not urgent. Like a party that comes to power and takes over the government, war brings in its own virtues and values to supplant those that rule during peace. Yet the effects of war have not been simple and totally adverse to freedom of thought.

Obviously the state of chronic emergency has increased the authority and power of governments. The revolutionary governments which established themselves in post-war situations calling for a strong hand found and perfected the means to make their power absolute, for they had the will to power at all costs and their illegitimacy imposed on them the logic of violence.[1] The democratic governments, when not

[1] See for the development of this theme *The Principles of Power* by G. Ferrero (London, 1949).

actually waging war nor building up national defence, had to deal with large and unfamiliar problems in the train of war, threatened within the gates by authoritarian elements that waited and worked for their expected failure. The limited increase in the power of democratic governments has accelerated the close organization of the sectional interests with which they have had to deal, and accelerated also the making of concessions to powerful demands for the sake of social unity; and with this has gone a tendency to stress traditional values and to give more official support to the authority and influence of established religion. This has been the democratic alternative to the totalitarian integration of all social organizations into the bureaucratic apparatus in the hands of the party in power. It has been in these circumstances that the progressive movement of enlightenment and emancipation reached in the democracies the late stages of its course, and is now being absorbed by a phase of rapidly developing social organization in which the very idea that deep divisions of opinion and of interests are inevitable and progressive has lost its orthodoxy and become a dangerous thought.

In the light of these recent events, it is instructive to look again at some part of the nineteenth-century background. The socialist sectaries of the nineteenth century, with the notable exception of Proudhon, were as authoritarian as the Protestant sectaries of the seventeenth century. The influential school of Saint-Simon, for example, proposed a planned society of producers ruled by scientists and technicians for the material and moral betterment of the masses, by whose labour, thus fertilized, all would live and prosper. Like Babeuf, Saint-Simon recognized that the workers had been left out of the benefits of 1789; and it is this exclusion of the workers from their share in the gains of any section of the middle classes, in support of whose interests they suffered in successive phases of revolutionary action throughout the nineteenth century, that bred the intransigence of communist politics. The right to freedom of thought admitted no connexion with the claim to bread. During the century, the workers were taught to trust only to power in their own hands, and the conquest of power became the essence of socialist doctrine. Marx provided justification for the head after experience had already established it in the heart. In 1906, Georges Sorel, in his influential *Réflexions sur la violence*, graved deeper the revolutionary lines of Marxism and idealized the anti-democratic intransigence of the workers. If they allowed themselves to be drawn into the parliamentary game, their political leaders would betray them; they would be insidiously enslaved and would lose their peculiar virtue and vigour. Marx founded his argument upon the necessary conditions of productive efficiency. Sorel injected into socialist theory the virulent objection of Nietzsche to utilitarian rationalism, the easy-going assumption of pacifist liberal democracy that the average appetites of average man can be happily satisfied by free markets, free elections, and popular education.

This moral and material nineteenth-century con-
demnation of modern democracy (as much romantic
as realist) is best looked at to-day within the perspective
of Tocqueville's view, standing as far back as 1835
and reflecting upon his observation of nascent democracy in Europe and in America. His constructive
criticism is still the most impressive warning of the
dangers inherent in the democratic movement, for he
foresaw that if the impatient critic of democracy
brought in equality by revolutionary violence he would
only be bringing to a definitive conclusion the tendency
of a sovereign people to pass into an unfelt servitude
to the 'sole, simple, providential, and creative power'
of their elected government. He foresaw that freedom
can only survive the irreversible trend towards equality
if it is saved by strong traditions upheld by powerful
convictions and reinforced by deliberate artifice. He
foresaw that if equality were introduced by an absolute
power or by revolution the possibility of freedom would
be extinguished: 'such a power does not destroy, but
it prevents existence'. That extinction of the source of
originality by prevenient policy is the most sinister of
all possibilities for human destiny. It is for that reason
that freedom of thought is to-day the most sacred of
causes.

In the later half of the nineteenth century at Harvard, American philosophical liberals, the founders of
Pragmatism, were re-affirming the faith of the British
philosophical radicals, derided on the Continent, and
re-affirming it with an historical and Darwinian outlook
in a diversity of fields of study and activity and with

vigorous insistence upon experimental freedom.[1] They were opposed to all authoritarian political and educational systems, to the technocracies of Saint-Simon and Comte as well as to the collectivism of revolutionary European socialists and to the rugged individualism of social Darwinians. It was a new liberal impulse, not less vigorous for being more subtle, complex, and theoretically better equipped than anything which had appeared in France or in England. But it was still engaged in the phase of emancipation.

On a long view, then, communism and fascism may be seen as extreme developments of a tendency within the democratic movement. They are developments which have challenged the democracies and made them conscious of the virtues as well as the weaknesses of their free institutions, for many were inclined at first to welcome and to idealize both communism and fascism when they came to power. Nineteenth-century liberalism had been so fatally abstract.[2] Representative government was frequently very bad government, and the citizen who had cast his vote was victim all

[1] *Evolution and the Founders of Pragmatism*, by Philip P. Wiener (Oxford, 1950).   .

[2] For example, this unexceptionable passage from Guizot's *History of the Origin of Representative Government in Europe*: 'It is . . . the character of that system, which nowhere admits the legitimacy of absolute power, to compel the whole body of citizens incessantly, and on every occasion, to seek after reason, justice, and truth, which should ever regulate actual power. The representative system does this, (1) by discussion, which compels existing powers to seek after truth in common; (2) by publicity, which places these powers when occupied in this search, under the eyes of the citizens; and (3) by the liberty of the press, which stimulates the citizens themselves to seek after truth, and to tell it to power.'

the same of events he was powerless to control. But now that the totalitarian alternative has been brought home to him by reliable report and by the witness of the refugee, he has a relish for the personal savour of freedom of thought, whether or not he appreciates its social utility.

Since Bury wrote, then, there has developed a world situation in which there are, on the one hand, the primitive or simplified totalitarian societies, and, on the other, the complex democracies with developing patterns of freedom and authority in partnership or tension in all the main fields of human activity. It is in these concrete contexts that the present state of freedom is to be studied and the future of freedom determined.

Bury dealt mainly with freedom of thought in religion because he said it could be taken as the thermometer for freedom of thought in general (p. 134). In so far as religion is no longer dominant, it is no longer a reliable index: at least, other pointers must be taken into account. It is in all the main fields of activity which require social organization and cultivate knowledge, thought, conscience, and opinion that the intricate and changing pattern of public and private initiative and control must be studied in modern society. For this purpose, education, the press and communications, parliament, and science must be added to religion. What follows is an attempt to delineate the main features of the situation in these fields in the west, seen in the perspective of developments since 1914.

RELIGION. Dissentient religious opinions, not secular thinking first disrupted Christendom. But dissent, in the main and certainly at the start, was seeking not freedom of thought but to oust and exterminate false and damnable rivals within a field of jurisdiction. The secular power itself (as in the hands of Elizabeth) was readier to make necessary concessions to dominant views, in order to impose uniformity for the sake of sound or easier government, than to admit diversity and practise toleration. It was the eventual impossibility of either sectarian domination or political uniformity in religion that founded conditions of toleration in England; and a common core of practical experience emerged in the principle of the separation of Church and State in most countries of the west, whatever the vicissitudes of national history. Where this happens, the Church may remain a powerful pressure group campaigning for its interests and influencing policy; and the Catholic Church has never abated its claims and still aspires to the restoration of Christendom, that is to say, to inspiring and ruling every activity of civilization. In Italy and even in France there are two nations following two traditions: there is Catholic Italy and Italy of the Risorgimento, and there is a reactionary Catholic France as well as the France of the republic and the secular school. In such conditions democracy is precarious, as the chequered modern history of France and Italy proves. A result of the Second World War has been the eclipse of the Catholic Church in those countries now dominated by communists, but beyond the frontiers of communism Rome is politically entrenched and enjoys enhanced moral prestige because of the fear of communism. Nevertheless, for all the inveterate paternalism of the Church, political catholicism in Europe to-day is democratic and progressive enough not to be an immediate threat to freedom. The test case is Italy, and there freedom of thought is all but inviolable and the Catholic Democratic Party shares with liberal political elements its governmental responsibility, if not its power.

In Britain, freedom of conscience can be tested at its weakest in the treatment of conscientious objection to military service, since it is not to be expected that in a time of national danger a minority of troublesome persons who refuse service will be tenderly dealt with, and in such emergencies the government is granted exceptional powers and normal liberties are suspended. Objectors who resisted conscription in the First World War were persecuted. When conscription was introduced the authorities made a determined and brutal attempt to break down the resistance, and public opinion was violently hostile to the C.O.s. When coercion failed and provoked protests, religious and moral objections to war were recognized and referred to tribunals. In the Second World War there were some 60,000 registered objectors, more than three times the number in the first war, and most of them were organized as members of one or other of the several pacifist associations. A Central Board for C.O.s was set up with local committees, as a voluntary effort to co-ordinate the associations and serve the interests of all C.O.s and represent them with the authorities. The principle of conscientious objection had been recognized and it was a question of detailed arrangements to give full and fair effect to it. In the first war many of the objectors were not pacifists but were politically hostile to the national policy, and no exemption was granted on other than pacifist grounds. In the second, there were far fewer political objectors and some of them gained exemption; for example, as socialists or Indian or Welsh nationalists. What was in question was not so much the ground of the objection nor its extent, as the depth of personal conviction which made the person prepared to defy the law if not given relief. The tribunals were instructed to judge the depth of personal conviction before reaching their decisions, whatever the opinion held, and to take into consideration the objector's predilections and scruples in deciding what work he should be directed to undertake. In short, the intention was to understand the point of view of the individual, and if possible to bring him into the war effort in a way that was both nationally useful and personally acceptable. The person who was determined not merely to resist conscription but also to bear witness against war as such was played off by this sympathetic approach, although the more determined did not escape punishment and the administration of the tribunals was far from being uniformly sympathetic or even fair. In sum, the principle of compulsion was carried much further in the second war, being applied to women, to industrial workers, and to fire-watching, but the principle of exemption for individuals who objected that their fundamental convictions were violated was fully respected, and the administration of this relief under the law set precedents for which history has no parallel.[1]

Within the totalitarian States, the heart of the situation has been, and is, the rivalry of Party and Church for the total allegiance of the citizen, the conscience of the individual. The historical separation of political order from religious or philosophical interpretation of the world, which issued in the liberal democratic State as a new value, was explicitly repudiated, not less by fascism than by communism. Mussolini described the Fascist state as a spiritual force 'which takes over all the forms of the moral and intellectual life of man', and as 'the soul of the soul'. 'Fascism, in short,' he wrote, 'is not only the giver of laws and the founder of institutions, but the educator and promoter of spiritual life. It wants to remake, not the forms of human life, but its content, man, character, faith. And to this end it requires discipline and authority that can enter into the spirits of men and there govern unopposed.' Clearly, where such a view prevails with the power to enforce it, all other authorities will be overruled and their teaching extirpated. But that is a counsel of perfection. The party which institutes the totalitarian State is a small minority, and just because it has undisputed mastery of all the means of influence by which opinions are formed, there is every reason

[1]For the first war, see *Conscription and Conscience*, by John W. Graham (Allen & Unwin, 1922). For the second, *Challenge of Conscience*, by Denis Hayes (Allen & Unwin, 1949).

not to upset people needlessly and to little purpose by disturbing deep-rooted sentiments. The Soviet Union established that lesson. The eradication of the Christian religion in totalitarian States is a long-term policy. Freedom of conscience is respected by the communists, as it was by the Nazis, to the extent that it is simply and solely freedom of religious worship and practice, the rights of the cult, and is compatible with absolute submission to the régime. Obviously, this simple principle is complicated from the outset by the need of the party to establish and perfect its control, which involves it in drastic interference with the Church in order to deal with resistant leaders, to remove education from clerical control, to supervise any religious teaching still allowed within the school, and to settle problems of church property and revenues. Clerical journals are also brought under close control, mainly and effectively by displacing unacceptable writers and substituting amenable journalists who have been given a course of political training. The Churches cannot without anomaly be integrated fully into the bureaucratic apparatus as are trade unions and other voluntary associations, but in fact that is the principle followed and that is what is virtually achieved. Both collaborators and resisters, of all degrees of compliance and heroism, are to be found in every situation which summons them, but under communism or fascism the Christian conscience cannot long remain a public witness against the policies, practices, or principles of the régime. Collaborators are flattered and promoted and used, but there can be no confidence in them because the principles of the two faiths are antithetic. Martin Bormann's secret memorandum produced at Nuremberg showed that the Nazis had no illusions about the German National Christians, than whom none could have made more haste nor run further in collaboration: it was recognized that all possible forms of Christianity were irreconcilable with nazism. In the Soviet Union, if the Orthodox Church has been reinstated it is solely as a cult under constant supervision, and if the cult does not wither away in due time but expands (and it is reported to be expanding), then measures will be taken to counter its attraction for the young. In Poland, formerly the most strongly held dominion of Rome, some five years of communist rule have driven the hierarchy to a last and hopeless stand.

In an interesting Preface contributed by the leader of the communist party in Italy to a translation of Voltaire's *Treatise on Toleration* published in 1949 in a popular series (the Preface was printed in the party paper *Unità* at the time), Signor Togliatti pays a tribute to the work of Voltaire and the rationalists as fighters for freedom of thought against the obscurantism and the fanaticism of the Church, but he regards toleration as a timely weapon in Voltaire's hands and not as a serious thesis; it is an ideal beyond practical politics, and in any case cannot be entertained in relation to a religious fanaticism the doctrinal basis of whose system of thought one does not respect, and he blames modern rationalist intellectuals for having sacrificed the gains of the past by the practice of an over-sophisticated

toleration which has allowed the clerical obscuran-
tists to renew the fight. Probably Signor Togliatti
refers to the abandonment of anti-clericalism by many
liberal rationalists in recent years, of whom his countryman Benedetto Croce is one of the most conspicuous.
This revision of their feelings and opinions about
Christianity by many liberals is so characteristic of the
time and so relevant to the theme of this book that
something more must be said about it. First, however,
it is worth recalling that not all rationalists have been
hostile to the Church. Saint-Simon, for example,
thought that in the long story of the exploitation of
man by man the Church had played a consistently
noble part, softening the rigour of the political and
economic order and pointing the way to emancipation
through its doctrine of human brotherhood and
equality before God: in his view, the Church had been
the one agent of civilization and the condition and
spring of progress. It is because it stands professedly for
brotherly love and the inviolability of the individual
conscience that many non-believers do not want to
see anything done to weaken the Church in the harsh
circumstances of the present time. The terrorism of
the Church, social and spiritual, belongs to a forgotten past. The Church is not nowadays hostile to
science nor to social reform, and the old rationalist
confidence in progress by means of enlightenment and
emancipation which inspired the fight against reaction
is less exciting in a diminished cause. The present
blend of the always necessary Christian compromise
with humanism is a particularly agreeable mixture

embodied in particularly impressive personalities. Psychologists, who have been the deadliest critics of the objective truth of religious dogmas, have also been witnesses to the necessity of religion. Jung, for example, reflecting upon his clinical experience and his observation of social psychology in Germany, sees in the leader figure of the political religions a substitute for the father whom most people cannot do without and whom the Church provides in a time-honoured and much safer and more satisfactory way. He is not alone in regarding old exploded myths as dried up watercourses, some of them deeply worn channels, to which the water may some day return, for they retain the underground connexion with the permanent psychic energies of men however often it is exposed by rationalist thought. The helpless nonentity of the individual in a mass industrial society, victim of agencies he does not know and cannot control, humiliates and terrifies him and releases destructive impulses which the demagogue knows only too well how to convert into the driving power of his new model. Kierkegaard said that only religion could save the individual from nonentity in the modern world; and the meaning of contemporary existentialism, atheist or Christian, is in its strenuous attempt by heroic measures to save individuality in modern mass society as the permanent creative principle of history.

Nevertheless, all such weighty reasons for second thoughts about Christianity do not make the religious archaism of the non-believer anything other than a counsel of fear and of despair. Whatever the historical role of the Church in civilizing barbarous Europe, the Christian to-day can have no realistic hope of influencing communism from within; and even if it were true that only Christian belief can save the open-eyed from defeatism, the unbeliever who founds his hopes upon that is a bankrupt who mechanically adds to his assets a nugatory nought.

EDUCATION. Bury's remark in his concluding paragraph that our methods of early education are founded on authority sounds old-fashioned to-day, for theory has taught us to be horrified by the idea, however unregenerate most of our schools remain in practice. Modern psychology has had its vast influence upon educational methods and ideals less by the light it has thrown on the learning process than by its revelation of the dynamics of human behaviour and development. Demonstration of the dangers of authoritarian influences in infancy made freedom the watchword, first of progressive experimental schools, and later, more or less modified, of general educational theory. This freedom has a positive basis: the young child must be enabled to become technically competent and socially acceptable in order to make a normal early adjustment of inner and outer demands. On the basis of acquired skills, in which no child is allowed to remain deficient, the school is built up into a happy community engaged in enjoyed activities, which all are eager to uphold and none is anxious to disrupt. This community is the great society in little and these activities are akin to the activities of real life, so that in the school the young are prepared for the world in the fundamental terms of achieved satisfactions on intelligible conditions, whether the material used is mainly book-learning or mainly practical activity. It is the free-spirited independent child on the side of society who can be taught to think for himself, not the crooked byronic rebel. It is the impulse to carry on a satisfactory going concern, bred and nursed in the interplay of individual (not least, inward) achievements and collective achievements, that is the origin of authentic public spirit, not the *esprit de corps* bound to a tradition. With this general type of educational policy in the schools goes the general social policy of making education available to all on a footing of social equality and of the particular type most suited to the needs and capacities of the individual child, so that the materials and methods used are those most likely to stimulate and maximize personal development. In none of all this is there anything that is fundamentally new; what is new is the theoretical hold and comprehensive insight which gives it universality and certainty, with the consequent social will to apply it. In this sense, these years have seen a liberal revolution in education which has affected all types of school and the most sacred educational traditions, even, for example, the Catholic schools and the Cartesian intellectualist educational tradition in France. The new ideas are leavening the whole lump with a basic humanism. They tend to justify if they do not compel the postponement of dogmatic issues to the later stages of education.

Whereas the new educational policy has come out of psychology and experimental schools and from the teachers themselves, the new social policy has come from the governments, pressed by the demand for equality and urged by the special need of modern industrial societies to make the most effective use of the nation's stock of intelligence and individual aptitude. This increasing strength of government initiative and control has raised the question of relations with other authorities in the field, the independent schools and, above all, the religious bodies. In each country the pattern of compromise is more or less complex and unstable, based on a political balance of forces liable to change. All that can be done here is to indicate the main influences at work in making the typical patterns which prevail to-day.

The Soviet Union was the first modern State to make education in secular State schools universally compulsory without alternative, and it may be assumed that this is the uniform pattern for all communist countries as soon as they can eliminate clerical control. The substitute for religious instruction and the ethos of the Church is of course Marxist ideology and the ethos of the socialist state. In the western democracies, there is, at least, toleration of denominational schools, at most, public payment of their cost. The Catholic parochial schools in America are regarded as more or less anomalous, for the secular schools of the public system, from which religious teaching is excluded, are jealously prized (as in France) as the foundation of the republic and the nursery of common citizen-ship.[1] Thus the vigorous and astute campaigning of the hierarchy to obtain the aid of public funds for education in American Catholic schools has been defeated, and the test cases carried to the Supreme Court have not provided any precedents for deviation from the strictest application of the rule of separation of Church and State.[2] All the same, there are strong currents of opinion which flow against the prevailing doctrine, for in the land of pioneer freedom in education it is not now so commonly believed that 'it is an immoral procedure for adults to seek to determine the future thought and conduct of the child'; and the decline of church attendance amongst the Protestant sects and the unsettlement of morals amongst young people have roused a feeling that religious teaching is a steadying factor and a national interest, and therefore not an improper object of public support.

In sum, the Catholic policy of segregation is unable to compete with the rising standard and cost of modern public systems of education, unless Catholic political power is great enough to enforce its claim to its own

[1] Professor I. L. Kandel, a famous American educator, sums up their tradition in education in these words: 'Because education is looked upon as a means of developing democratic ideals and social equality, there is a tendency to regard the public school as the sole agency to which this task can be entrusted and to look upon the private school as somewh a un-American in character and as the only justification fo its existence the opportunity to experiment.'

[2] See *American Freedom and Catholic Power*, by Paul Blanshard (1949) ; *Cornerstones of Religious Freedom in America*, by Joseph L. Blau (1949); *The American Tradition in Religion and Education*, by R. Freeman Butts (1950); *The Attack upon the American Secular School*, by V. T. Thayer (1951).

schools at the public cost, as in Belgium, for example; and then the effect of duplication is seriously to embarrass the development of the public system on universally approved modern lines. It is not a simple issue of rights of conscience within a common society: it is the stubborn challenge of an alien authoritarian régime whose claims are unbounded even when limited by *le tact des choses possibles*.

Thus the schools of Europe and the western world are all more or less strongly coloured by Marxism, Christianity, Judaism, or democratic nationalism, save the exceptional few which manage to be free and progressive by being studiously pagan, pacifist, internationalist, or otherwise unconventional, a more or less valuable effort liable to the disadvantage of producing social misfits. It is not the school (nor the university) that changes a society, for a society takes care to perpetuate itself through the school, although it has also to reproduce itself through the less calculable new generation. But it is not the transmission of a positive and cherished tradition that is illiberal; the illiberal thing is the teaching, or the suggestion, that alternatives, actual and possible, are evil or contemptible.

The problem in the modern universities of the western democracies is the problem of intellectual and moral coherence, the problem of the consequences of freedom, a problem aggravated by the increasing number of students and the increasing specialization and segregation of studies. University teachers and administrators and others are awake to the problem and there have been notable theoretical contributions to the question and some concrete experiments. It is safe to say that no dogmatic scheme or theoretical synthesis is likely to rule over the republic of learning in the democracies in place of the dethroned queen of the sciences, theology. For a long time to come there will remain the alternative theoretical interpretations; and, of not less importance, the actual coherence, the concrete synthesis of society with its practical problems and achievements, will increasingly guide the orientation of studies. But where society is bitterly divided it does not need the enthronement of dogma to imperil academic freedom. President Truman's Commission on Higher Education in 1946 strongly recommended 'that a move be launched and carried through by national organizations of laymen to acquaint the American people, including the teaching profession, with the practical implications of academic freedom and the need for championing it as a fundamental national policy'. The violent animosity against liberal views which has gained ground in America since then has included university teachers of the highest integrity amongst its victims.

PARLIAMENT. Parliament, and particularly the British Parliament, has long been the hope and home of freedom. Here the nation in little freely settled the common affairs by open debate. Here ministers of the crown took responsibility for all that their subordinates did under the law in the administration of public business. Here authority could be challenged and everything dragged into the light of day. Here the initiatives of government had to pass through the mill of jealous scrutiny and informed criticism. Here individual grievances and private proposals were voiced and heard. Generations of reformers, and even agitators, lived by faith in a fully representative Parliament. Yet none of the free institutions of political democracy has come under such heavy fire of criticism in our time, and in the totalitarian countries it has fallen back into being what it was under previous despotisms, a purely consultative assembly. In the long run competence proves a better title to power than legitimacy, and free elections do not prevent politicians from fooling the people. The general election of 1918 in Britain and the government that was returned shook the confidence of many democrats. In France, the chronic instability of the administration went far to discredit the Third Republic before the collapse in the war. The campaigns of rival interests for favourable tariffs threatened to make nonsense of politics in the Weimar Republic before the days of Hitler. Mussolini was not the first nor the only post-war dictator to make the need for government the reasonable excuse for sweeping away the boast of democracy.

The ordinary man, even if he feels that he is adequately represented in parliament, probably does not feel that his representative has any opportunity of being party to the big decisions by which his destiny is ruled, which he will suspect are not taken openly on the floor of the House but behind closed doors by representatives of powerful financial and industrial interests. As long ago as 1913, Woodrow Wilson in his election campaign speeches made a principal theme of the eclipse of Congress and demanded a return to open debate and the full light of information on all that touched the public interest.[1] About the same time, Graham Wallas in *The Great Society* was writing a scathing account of the factitious character of a debate in the House of Commons. His point, however, was the opposite of Wilson's, for he was trying to show that effective discussion and the influence of mind on mind cannot take place on the floor of the House in full debate, and to argue that the pretence of it should be abandoned and parliamentary procedure recognized for what it is, a method of testing strength and registering the will of the disciplined majority. The locus of power, that is, of effective decision, had shifted from parliament to the party caucus—or, as Professor James Burnham will have it, to the bureaucratic controllers of industry.

The House of Commons remains, in spite of the necessary party machines, the nation in little, and its public debates both express and form public opinion upon the questions of the day. President Wilson's ideal was formed on the simpler model of nineteenth-century British liberalism, but his point was valid, and Graham Wallas was only probing to find ways and means of giving full effect to it in terms of modern efficiency, with his own magnificent confidence in the

[1]'The concern of patriotic men is to put our government again on its right basis, by substituting the popular will for the rule of guardians, the processes of common counsel for those of private arrangement. In order to do this, a first necessity is to open the doors and let in the light on all affairs which the people have a right to know about.' Woodrow Wilson, *The New Freedom*, p. 109 (London, 1913).

possibility and the value of independent original thinking everywhere if the right conditions for it were understood and provided. The inhibition of independent thinking is organized with devilish efficiency by the rulers of states who make a monopoly of initiative, and the promotion of it can be organized not less carefully and intelligently by those who believe in its beneficent utility. It requires positive efforts and a sustained national faith to make sure that independent individual thinking is encouraged and facilitated and that adequate relevant information is available wherever policies are made, and that such policies and the responsibility for them have the requisite publicity. The fact that this aspect of society has become an object of attention and of organized study is itself some assurance that freedom of thought will mean thinking to some purpose.[1]

PRESS. Tocqueville, scrutinizing all the means by which it might be hoped that the drift to absolute State power inherent in the tendency to equality would be countered, put his confidence in the press as the democratic instrument of liberty, because the individual by that means could make a stir, call for help, and appeal to the conscience of the nation or of mankind.

[1]Following the report of a select committee in 1946, the House of Commons re-organized its library and added research and reference divisions, with competent staff charged 'to assist members in their researches'.

For theoretical analysis, see *Man and Society in an Age of Reconstruction*, by Karl Mannheim (Kegan Paul, 1940) and *The Analysis of Political Behaviour*, by Harold D. Lasswell (Kegan Paul, 1948).

As Erskine put it in his defence of Paine, 'other liberties are held *under* governments, but the liberty of opinion keeps governments themselves in due subjection to their duties'. It was the central belief of the nineteenth-century liberal creed that the appeal to reason would prevail through the freedom of the press. This belief was the product of a homogeneous, educated ruling class, and left out of account the mass basis of modern industrial societies which the pressure for equality was making the big factor in politics. The new demagogues believed just as firmly in the power of public opinion, but they recognized that it could be organized and manipulated, and that even if they did not come to power by capturing it, once in power, the illegitimacy of their rule could be varnished with a favourable popular opinion quickly manufactured.

The power of politically directed propaganda was proved during the First World War, mainly by the effectiveness of the British use of it; and after the Bolshevik revolution the new régime set up the Comintern for defensive and offensive propaganda in their struggle for survival in a hostile world. It is ironical that it should have been the English fighting to make the world safe for democracy who gave the first convincing demonstration of the modern power of propaganda. Hitler's classical account in *Mein Kampf* showed how the lesson was learned. In a favourable situation even the enemy could be made to think what one wanted him to think. In a situation of total anxiety repetition of the simple appropriate idea finds access to all minds and thereafter the idea colours all thinking.

To spell out large and plain for the less literate the right and the wrong, the true and the false, what to love and what to hate, was the necessary counterpart of the esoteric doctrine of the initiates, and served to move and to fortify the masses as the ideology and the vertical stiffening of the party discipline inspired and upheld the *élite*. Man is a rational animal, and doctrine and slogan provide at different intellectual levels the inoculation which gives immunity from more active or more restless thinking, and keeps the citizen or the party-member confident, purposive, and responsive.

In the democracies, what monopoly there has been in the means of communication has been either in the autocratic control of newspaper chains or in the public control of broadcasting. The report of the Royal Commission on the Press in Britain, published in 1949, found no serious continuing tendency to monopoly and no undue pressure from big advertisers, but very great differences in the standard of truth and impartiality. The recommendation of the Commission that the press should itself establish a general council to safeguard the freedom of the press and to encourage the growth of the sense of public responsibility and public service amongst those professionally engaged in journalism, was in line with post-war developments in other professional organizations, including trade unions, which have been required to take responsibility for giving shape and effect to public policy in addition to serving the professional interests of their members. This form of partnership is the democratic alternative to integration into the bureaucratic apparatus of the

State, and upon its success depends the future of free institutions.

In the U.S.A., merger and monopoly seem to have gone further. Ten states have no city with competing daily newspapers, and in the last decades newspapers and weeklies have disappeared by the thousand.[1] One or two cases of large-scale bribery of the press by industrial corporations have been exposed in recent years. Newspaper attacks on persons and associations are frequently savage, unscrupulous, and damaging. This question of defamation has blown big and explosive in the wake of the loyalty investigations excited by the fear of communists, which has given scope to those who hate all radical and liberal opinions and tendencies in the country. The length to which persecution has gone is a profound challenge to American democratic sentiment.

Broadcasting may be a public monopoly, as in Britain, a complex of licensed private agencies under some public regulation and supervision, as in the U.S.A., or a public system in competition with private agencies, exercising control over them, as in Canada, or subject to independent public control, as in Australia. The patterns are various, and there is none that is universally best, regardless of local conditions and problems. Nor could it ever be possible to have all the virtues and none of the defects and deficiencies of both the public monopoly and the open field. An established

[1] *The First Freedom*, by Morris Ernst (New York, 1946); also the *Report of the Commission on Freedom of the Press* (University of Chicago Press, 1947).

system is likely to be basically adapted to local conditions and needs, and is more likely to be improved for the purpose of freedom of expression, or for any purpose, by applying remedies for proved defects than by revolutionary change. That is the principle of the conclusions and recommendations of the 1949 Broadcasting Committee's Report (H.M.S.O., January 1951). There is always a case against monopoly, but the B.B.C. is charged with ensuring freedom of expression, has declared that its highest duty is the search for truth, and works under constant and close public watch. Experience shows that freedom of thought in the shape of minority opinion may be safer in such hands than by taking its luck in the rough field of open competition for mass interest. In any case, the most fundamental principle of all is that the organization of broadcasting shall remain an open question of public interest and not be locked away in the tool-chest of the government.[1]

Although there is no censorship of the press in the democracies in peace time, books are liable to be seized and destroyed on the ground of obscenity, and publishers, authors, booksellers, and librarians are liable to be prosecuted and punished on this ground. Several cases in recent years have shown that the law of obscene libel may be arbitrarily administered and

[1]On this section, see: *Propaganda and Promotional Activities: an annotated bibliography*, by Lasswell, Casey, and Smith (Minnesota, 1935); *Propaganda, Communication, and Public Opinion: a comprehensive reference guide*, by Smith, Lasswell, and Casey (Princeton, 1946); *Free Speech in the U.S.*, by Z. Chafee, Jr. (Harvard, 1941); *Radio, Television, and Society*, by C. A. Siepmann (Oxford, 1950).

effect the suppression of serious and useful works.[1] There are still pockets of obscurantism and certain hard seams of resistance, but for the most part the whole subject of sex has been flooded with discussion, and information on sex problems and on birth control is made widely available under official auspices.

Colonial peoples naturally use the press to conduct their agitation for the realization of their nationalist aspirations, and naturally they come up against the government. The Seventh Imperial Press Conference (1950) thoroughly examined the question of the Colonial Press Laws, and proposed machinery for closer co-operation between the Empire Press Union and the Colonial Office, with the object of securing responsible publication and avoiding repressive legislation. Apart from the question of dependent peoples is the problem of political parties which advocate violence and owe allegiance to a foreign power. There is nothing in democratic theory which requires that they shall be tolerated. But there are weighty reasons for the maximum practical toleration of radical ideas which are incitements to action, unless and until they constitute a 'clear and present danger'. This is in the liberal tradition and there are many reasons why it is sound practice, not least because the party in question can hardly fail to represent, however crudely, some vital interest or some aspect of truth, indeed some deficiency in the recognized alternatives.

[1]See *The Banned Books of England*, by Alec Craig (Allen & Unwin, 1937) and *Above all Liberties* by Alec Craig (Allen & Unwin, 1942).

SCIENCE. The life-blood of modern industrial civilization is science, and science as the most reliable and socially useful result of organized thought is a main consideration in concern for intellectual freedom. The scientist himself is not necessarily concerned about intellectual freedom nor even aware of its conditions in relation to his own work. The idea that the scientist stands out for freedom of thought against authority is a story-book idea, a high-light on the romantic past. Nor is the agency which employs the modern scientist necessarily concerned for freedom of thought or aware of its conditions in relation to the science or the phase of research in question. In no field is public faith in the social utility of freedom of thought and public insistence on the quest and the respect for its conditions more needed at the present time than in the rapidly developing organization of scientific research. Between the wars, scientists complained of frustration for lack of the financial means of large-scale research, because the tempo of industrial expansion had been slowed down by monopolies and the economic slump. It seemed that the unlimited social possibilities of science could only be realized in societies which had the vision and daring to throw down the political and economic barriers by direct action and set the scientists to work by providing the means and utilizing the results. The war itself had this effect, and after the war the economic plight of Britain ensured that public money would be forthcoming on a much more adequate scale for the training of scientists and the equipment of research. Of course it was the applications of the results of major researches in nuclear physics which were the most spectacular and expensive of the projects sponsored by governments during the war, and the most far-reaching in consequences. These researches had been far advanced before the war broke out and were linked discoveries, the product of free intercommunication and worldwide scientific collaboration. The conditions under which scientists in this field now work are far different.

Even in fields of research which are not secret and under government surveillance, the modern scale of equipment and personnel and the internal subdivision and technical specialization of the work have transformed the conditions of scientific thinking. The demand for results when large sums of money have to be found increases the tension between theory and practice, the need for fundamental research and the exigency of pressing wants and hopes. The Lysenko affair was a dramatic instance of this tension, which can only be resolved by an instructed and mature faith in the methods of theoretical science: a scientist who has achieved public prestige and influence may be of greater immediate social utility than a better scientist. In the western democracies, it will be the scientific leader himself in a position of responsibility who will be tempted to justify himself by results and to play them up without due regard for the second thoughts and doubts and infinite patience which have distinguished the pioneers working at leisure and alone or with a few elect colleagues: for the conditions of selection may be increasingly unfavourable to the genuinely original scientist. And the more efficient the specialist is in his indispensable technical capacity the less is he likely to be able to think about the problem itself and the development of the science as a whole. The increasing abstractness of science (in which progress lies) and the increasing complexity of the theoretical techniques employed, which have to be taken on trust, tend to remove the scientist both from the actual world and from the philosophic level into the most sterile region of all. These are some of the recognized tendencies induced by the external conditions and the internal dynamics of modern scientific research, and which call for public awareness as well as for the attention of scientists and for remedial policies in the field of higher education. The emergence of outstanding scientific genius in the field of physics in the recent past is no assurance for the future. This tree of knowledge is a shy bearer that does well in certain sheltered conditions, and not much is yet known about its hardy cultivation on a large scale in the open. In this as in other respects the dangers that are recognized so plainly as existing beyond the 'iron curtain' are crude forms of a tendency insidiously present in the necessary conditions of modern society.

Whereas in the physical sciences access to information in certain fields has become restricted by official secrecy, historical materials have never before been so freely and fully available to the student. Contemporary archives are overflowing, and the student can hardly see the wood for the trees.

.   .   .   .   .

In 1905 Dicey summed up the emancipation and enlightenment achieved in the nineteenth century by saying that England enjoyed 'a freedom of thought and of discussion more complete than has ever permanently existed among the whole people of any country known to us by history'. He did not think the consequences were all that the prophets had expected. 'Mill and others held, and with truth, that vigorous persecution, either legal or social, may destroy the capacity for free thought. They thence concluded that absolute freedom would stimulate originality and individuality. This inference is of most dubious validity.' He was content to note that freedom of thought was associated with the disintegration of beliefs, religious, moral, political, and economic, because it showed up the disagreements and inconsistencies; and to express the opinion that freedom served to indulge man's natural laziness and imitativeness rather than to stimulate his inventiveness. He misrepresented Mill, who, like Tocqueville, had feared that with the freedom and equality of all a creeping paralysis of 'Chinese stagnation and immobility' would overspread the whole of society unless 'all human resources' were employed to provide against it before it was too late. The provisions Mill looked to were legal forms and institutions rooted in the national habit and character and justified by reason and experience. Can the problem, however, be rightly thought of in terms of safeguarding minorities and independent thinkers? Is not the free exchange of goods in the open market more of a condition than an analogy for the free exchange of ideas? Does not the

emergence of the commercial corporation, the trade
union, and the political party (to say nothing of the
national State), with their organized monopolies and
competing mass appeals as the dominant social reali-
ties, put out of business the free intellectual, dealing
in creative ideas and representing no interest but the
disinterestedness of discursive intelligence? It was to
take account of the new social dynamics and to
introduce into the working of organized thought, in
gear with organized will, the psychological conditions
of intellectual efficiency and fertile invention that
Graham Wallas explored the field again and communicated a new impulse and a new direction to study
of the social problem. Nevertheless, it is not reduced,
and never can be, to a mere problem of organization;
it remains in part a political struggle, a victory to be
fought for. This is exemplified by the argument of
Professor Laski's spirited restatement of the case for
freedom of thought in his *Liberty in the Modern State*
(1930, revised *Pelican* edition, 1937). New thought,
he argues, threatens the holders of privilege, and
therefore freedom of thought has to fight for the overthrow of privilege; it is the cause of the rising element
in society. On the other hand, since new thought does
come from vigorous rising elements with whom the
future lies, history proves the futility of attempting
to smother such springing vitality and plug such
spirting forces. If the balloon is pricked it might as
well be slashed, and unfortunately the argument is
quite as strong in warning a totalitarian régime against
the slightest relaxation as in encouraging a liberal one

to gain courage by conviction. And, again unfortunately, liberalism has something to lose by too
powerful a conviction and too rooted a habit of assimi-
lative patience and too resourceful a passion for
synthesis: Jean-Paul Sartre has described how the
humanistic belief in democratic tolerance and progress
which was the formative ideal of three successive
generations in France removed the very idea that there
could be evil and error which had to be discerned and
denounced and fought. Under the head of appease-
ment, our generation has learned painfully to be
hypersensitive to this weakness, which has not cured
but complicated the disease.

The bewildering plurality of standpoints and contexts confuses the issue until we go back to first
principles, and first principles in this case are drawn
from historical experience. In England the appeal
against absolute government was to the restraint of
custom (and, more vaguely, of natural law) enforced
by the sanction of rebellion. On the other hand, the
claim to absolute power founds itself upon the justification of an absolute purpose, whether it is the 'rule
of the saints' in seventeenth-century England, or the
rule of the party hierarchy in contemporary Russia,
or the rule of the philosophers in Plato's Republic.
The liberal ideal of the restraint of power (perhaps a
mere knave-proof and fool-proof constitution) seems
negative defeatism or weak optimism in comparison
with the positive and daring bid of the absolutists to
mould man in the image of some sacred ideal by a
rigorous discipline without which he is wretched.

Nevertheless, with the development in the nineteenth century of methods of science and rational investigation and of methods of representative government and democratic association, the idea of seeking truth and justice in common by public and objective procedures offered an ideal as absolute as that of philosophers or theologians, to be attained by a rigorous discipline that was not servitude but rational freedom and which was not only less open to reasonable dissent but was actually itself a test of good faith and the rational qualification for authority. By these means both interests and opinions could be modified and brought nearer to a common measure, not by the dubious and depressing arrangements of expediency and compromise but by raising them to an objective standard.

This historical introduction of freedom of thought as a universal and necessary social ideal, with its operational definition in terms of public procedures, is the one permanent social foundation for all legitimate building. If in pursuing the methods of science and of democracy both thought and interests have become highly organized and closely specialized, those are the new conditions and the new problems for freedom. Although these forms of organization are forms of social order and control, they are compatible with cultural and moral disintegration, since specialization and segregation produce it, and since the methods of science and of democracy do not of themselves solve ultimate problems of truth and value, and leave a margin with ample room for widely divergent views, in which absolutists may become dominant. (Perhaps there was never more need for the well-equipped, detached intellectual to work in this margin, and never less social and educational provision for him.) The scale of organization, the rate of change, the range of every social problem demand strong and competent government and over-riding common social purpose, and this encourages the absolutist, whatever his complexion, to hope that in an emergency the easier way of drastic simplification can be made the preferred alternative. Freedom of thought, like soil conservation, is a long-term policy, a faith in historical man, an imaginative concern for human destiny. More immediate satisfactions are probably to be gained by sacrificing it, but the quick-returns permanently impoverish the cultural soil.

Social progress is no longer possible by *laissez-faire*; it is a difficult possibility which depends on our capacity for rational control, and rational control, as Ruth Benedict has pointed out, is most endangered by those deep assumptions and dominant values with which a society is most sensitively identified and of which it is quick to resent and repel criticism. Such rational control is not merely nor mainly government control; it is rather a social purpose to which government as one particular social function is responsive. Such a social purpose is at the present time neither totally unformed and unmeaning nor unchallenged: this growing point of society needs the sap of free discussion.

Although the case for freedom of thought rests

basically on its permanent social utility, those who demand it for themselves are those who know how to interpret and share and how to promote their own experience, and who delight to participate in the experience of others, with no nonsense about authority.

BIBLIOGRAPHY

General

LECKY, W. E. H., *History of the Rise and Influence of the Spirit of Rationalism in Europe*, 2 vols. (originally published in 1865). WHITE, A. D., *A History of the Warfare of Science with Theology in Christendom*, 2 vols., 1896. ROBERTSON, J. M., *A Short History of Free-thought, Ancient and Modern*, 2 vols., 1906. [Comprehensive, but the notices of the leading freethinkers are necessarily brief, as the field covered is so large. The judgements are always independent.] BENN, A. W., *The History of English Rationalism in the Nineteenth Century*, 2 vols., 1906. [Very full and valuable.]

Greek Thought

GOMPERZ, TH., *Greek Thinkers* (English translation), 4 vols. (1901–12).

English Deists

STEPHEN, LESLIE, *History of English Thought in the Eighteenth Century*, vol. i, 1881.

French Freethinkers of the Eighteenth Century

MORLEY, J., *Voltaire; Diderot and the Encyclopaedists; Rousseau* (see above, Chapter VI).

Rationalistic Criticism of the Bible
(Nineteenth Century)

Articles in *Encyclopaedia Biblica*, 4 vols. DUFF, A., *History of Old Testament Criticism*, 1910. CONYBEARE, F. C., *History of New Testament Criticism*, 1910.

NOTE.—Bury's bibliography is kept intact to show the main sources he relied on. More recent works are cited in my footnotes to his text and to the Epilogue. I would add three others: a study of the Roman idea of liberty, *Libertas as a Political Idea at Rome during the Late Republic and Early Principate*, by Ch. Wirszubski, C.U.P., 1950; a study of the establishment of the moral authority of the mediaeval church, A.D. 400–800, *The First Europe*, by C. Delisle Burns, Allen & Unwin, 1947; and, for the view of a Christian historian to-day, Professor H. Butterfield's Riddell Lectures, *Christianity in European History*, O.U.P., 1951.— H.J.B.

Persecution and Inquisition

LEA, H., *A History of the Inquisition of the Middle Ages*, 3 vols., 1888; *A History of the Inquisition of Spain*, 4 vols., 1906. HAYNES, E. S. P., *Religious Persecution*, 1904. For the case of Ferrer see ARCHER, W., *The Life, Trial and Death of Francisco Ferrer*, 1911, and MCCABE, J., *The Martyrdom of Ferrer*, 1909.

Toleration

RUFFINI, F., *Religious Liberty* (English translation), 1912. The essays of L. LUZZATTI, *Liberty of Conscience and Science* (Italian), are suggestive.

Index